THE GUITARIST'S SURVIVAL GUIDE

BY KAI NAREZO & SCOTT WOLF

FLAMENCO EXPLAINED THE GUITARIST'S SURVIVAL GUIDE

Cover Design and Photos by Tara Stewart

Printed in the United States of America
First Printing, 2018
www.FlamencoExplained.com

ISBN: #978-1-5323-6264-4

Why This Book?

There have never been more resources available to someone wanting to learn flamenco guitar – millions of videos, books of transcriptions, and many good books on flamenco technique. So why write another book about flamenco guitar? The short answer is that there is so much more to flamenco than solo guitar pieces, and to my knowledge no one has tackled the language of flamenco in its totality. This aspect is too often treated as an "unteachable" mystery, and yet I believe that the fundamentals of flamenco guitar playing can be taught – this includes both solo playing and accompaniment.

Flamenco is a folk music. As a guitarist, it is too easy to focus on the virtuosity and overlook those elements that make flamenco what it is. As in any other style of music, technique is a means to an end, and is meaningless without an understanding and appreciation of flamenco's roots and traditions.

Understanding *compás* (this word is all over this book, so now might be a good time to see the Glossary) and having good technique is the first step. Many students come equipped with a technical foundation, but without a clear idea of what to do when confronted with *cante* (song) or *baile* (dance). From the outside, it is often a mystery how flamenco dancers communicate with the musicians, without a single word spoken, as well as how the musicians communicate amongst themselves. In fact flamenco is simply another language, and the good news is that it can be learned.

Just like any other style of music, not everything can be communicated in flamenco without some rehearsal. When you see a professional performance, while there may be elements of improvisation, most often what you are seeing is a well choreographed performance. In a *tablao*, as in a jazz club, musicians and dancers who may have never worked or rehearsed together, use the language of flamenco to communicate and perform as if they had been working together all their lives.

One of the other benefits of really understanding this language is that it allows you to "improvise" in flamenco – that is, to use all of the material you have at your disposal to construct a solo on the fly, in much the same way that a jazz player might use licks to construct a solo. You need a solid foundation in time and structure, and you need to understand where the music comes from (usually in terms of the *cante* - see glossary). As you'll see, this will give you the freedom to express yourself in a style that from the outside can seem rigid and constrained, but that like jazz or the blues is simply another form of expression with its own history and traditions.

For those who grow up surrounded by flamenco there is no mystery – the musical language of flamenco is as simple and clear to them as their native tongue. Not having this advantage myself, I learned by embracing all the elements of flamenco: the dance, the cante, the *palmas*, and the guitar. Additionally, I listened to every recording I could get my hands on. Working in the *tablao* environment, I found fluency among these elements. This is the flamenco that I try to impart to my students, and now to you in this book.

A few years ago I started working with a new student, Dr. Scott Wolf (DMA), who was surprised that we were covering many of the elements of flamenco he had been told were not teachable. He convinced me that there was a need for a book like this and offered to help translate some of the concepts with some novel (and, I believe, extremely helpful) ideas about notation. We hope this helps you to better understand the language of flamenco.

Kai Narezo

Table of Contents

About the Authors

Kai Narezo

I learned flamenco the old-fashioned way – at the feet of great guitarists first in NY and then inevitably in Spain. I then spent hundreds of hours playing for dance classes and for every

singer who would let me get close enough. I was lucky to have some amazing teachers - Dennis Koster in NY, who gave me a thorough foundation in what we now think of as old-school flamenco, and then in Granada, Spain, where I lived for two years, with Juan Fernandez, who brought me up to date and kicked my ass, and then later some truly amazing time with Enrique de Melchor who I never dreamed I'd actually get to study with.

Once I had already been making a living playing for a few years I decided I wanted to learn how to read and write music and expand my ears, so I got a BEST scholarship to Berklee College of Music, in Boston, had the time of my life, and learned the skills that would let me communicate with other musicians (you guys!). Of course to make a living I played flamenco – gigging, teaching, and spending another thousand or so hours playing for dance classes, mostly for the legendary Ramon De Los Reyes (who bought me my first black suit).

Berklee didn't turn me into a jazzer (they eventually gave up), but it showed me that flamenco as an art form stands on its own, and helped me share my ideas with other players, who in turn teach me. A musical life worth living (for me) happens this way.

While I'm a bit of an expatriate as an American flamenco guitarist and composer, I'm at home in flamenco. That is why I want to share this amazing art form with you.

Scott Wolf

Scott Wolf is known for his performing, teaching, arranging, and for his highly acclaimed podcast, All Strings Considered.

He earned his doctorate in classical guitar studying with Scott Tennant at the University of Southern California. Before his move to Los Angeles, Wolf received his master's degree with Eliot Fisk at New England Conservatory, and a bachelor's degree studying with Randy Pile at U.C. San Diego. A

flamenco aficionado, Wolf began flamenco guitar while living in Spain in 2003, and has continued his flamenco studies in the U.S. with Grisha Goryachev, Adam Del Monte, Juanito Pascual, and Kai Narezo. Over the last several years, the Loyola Marymount Guitar Festival, the GFA Symposium in Los Angeles, and the University of Southern California have invited Wolf to give his sought-after 'Flamenco for Classical Guitarists' workshops, and Scott Tennant and Adam Del Monte frequently invite him as a guest instructor for their private studios at USC.

A dedicated performing artist and chamber musician, Wolf most recently accompanied Susan Egan at the Huntington Library alongside Dr. Steve Cook. During the 2014 Guitar Foundation of America, Wolf was a guest player in a lecture given by Dr. Alexander Dunn on Turina's life and works. He also performs regularly with soprano Janelle DeStefano and Wendy Castellanos in the Composer Alive Series, playing the music of Manuel De Falla. Wolf was also a featured soloist with the La Jolla Symphony and Chorus in Golijov's Oceana, and played mandolin in UC San Diego's New Music Palimpsest playing Carter's Liumen.

Wolf is avid arranger of solo and chamber music; his work can be heard performed by such notable groups as the Grammy Winning L.A.G.Q., the USC Guitar Ensembles, and the Whittier Guitar Ensemble. His arrangements can be found from Les Productions d'OZ, Seconda Prattica, and others, and links to all of these can be found on his website: www.scottwolfguitar.com

A dedicated teacher, Scott Wolf serves on the faculty of Oxnard College where he directs the music program.

Explanation of Symbols

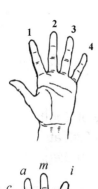

Fingers on the left hand are numbered

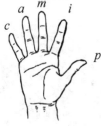

Fingers on the right hand are given letters corresponding to their names in Spanish

① ② ③ ④ ⑤ ⑥   String numbers from treble to bass

↑   *Rasgueado* downstroke (towards the floor)

↓   *Rasgueado* upstroke (towards the ceiling)

$\uparrow$ *m* *a*   Downstroke with *m* and *a* simultaneously

$\uparrow$ *m* *(a)*   Downstroke with either *m* or *a*

$\uparrow$ *p*   Thumb downstroke from wrist for *alzapúa*

Golpe above the first string with *a*

Golpe below the sixth string with *i*

Open-handed slap of the strings with the right hand

Compás (Rhythm)

The twelve-beat *compás* is as much a cycle as it is a closed "measure" of music. Each *compás* flows into the next, and each *compás* has two main arrival points: beats 3 and 10. You will see that both rhythmically and harmonically/melodically the music drives towards these beats. The infinite variety of ways of driving towards these two beats is what makes flamenco so fascinating (and occasionally confounding).

At its most basic, the *compás* is simply a frame into which we must fit the music. As we get deeper into it, however, we see that the harmony frequently changes on beats 3 and 10. We can hear this very clearly in the first few *compáses* of a Solea *letra*, as the guitar accompaniment moves from E to F on beat 3 and resolves back to E on beat 10.

We're going to start by looking at the 12-beat *compás* and the two most common ways the accents are arranged – with accents on 12, 3, 6, 8 and 10, and with accents on 12, 3, 7, 8, and 10. This is best understood by simply clapping on every beat below, and accenting the beats in bold, larger type (this is actually your first lesson in *palmas*, the rhythmic hand-claps that are the percussive foundation of flamenco). For more on *palmas*, go to *FlamencoExplained.com*. You'll hear that the first *compás* sounds very much like a measure of $\frac{3}{4}$ followed by a measure of $\frac{6}{8}$, while the second version may feel a bit less familiar.

You may wonder why we are starting here on beat 12 instead of beat 1. This is more of a semantic argument than a practical one, but if it makes you feel better, just think of it like a clock. We start our day at 12, not at 1, and it turns out that this terminology has been used for as long as flamenco has been counted. Coming from the Western musical tradition, you might be tempted to call the first beat in the cycle beat 1, rather than beat 12, because it feels like a downbeat. This will only cause confusion in communicating with other flamenco performers.

Accent Pattern 1:

‖: **12** 1 2 **3** 4 5 **6** 7 **8** 9 **10** 11 :‖

Accent Pattern 2:

‖: **12** 1 2 **3** 4 5 6 **7** **8** 9 **10** 11 :‖

- Once you are comfortable repeating each of these patterns, try alternating the two.

- You might also try clapping these at tempos ranging from 40 to 250 BPM.

- If you really want to get fancy, clap twice for each beat (i.e., subdivide into eighth notes).

Notating Compás in This Book

Our system for notating the twelve-beat cycle is slightly different than other texts. This is an attempt to make the look of the music notation closer to what it actually feels like to play it. This list explains how our notation works:

• When you encounter the twelve-beat cycle in our text, each system (line of music) will represent one full twelve-beat compás.

• Quarter notes will always be used as the beat.

• Important beats - often these are beats 12, 3, 6, 8, and 10 - will be marked in the notation to help you navigate each cycle. These are the numbers that you will see in the example notation below.

• When you see a number embedded in the staff, it identifies the beat immediately following it. The arrows in the example below illustrate this.

Feeling Compás on the Guitar

This exercise will help you get a sense for what the twelve-beat *compás* feels like on the guitar.

Using only the index finger of your right hand, and playing downstrokes on the downbeats and upstrokes on the upbeats, listen to how the music flows away from the A-chord and then returns. In time you will hear these four variations as slightly different ways of expressing the same idea – the move away on beat 3 and the resolution on beat 10. In flamenco, collecting and composing licks that resolve back to beat 10 is a way of life, and in many cases you will recognize a certain player simply by hearing the way she or he plays from beats 7 to 10.

You will experience different feels or grooves as you play different tempos, but the basic math of the *compás* remains the same. You can expect to play these types of phrases in various keys with the same results.

As we slow down the *compás* you may begin to hear that beat 12 doesn't always sound like a downbeat. This is normal, and as we get into Soleares, beat 12 will all but disappear as the downbeat, while the arrangement of accents otherwise remains the same.

This example also gives you a chance to get comfortable with the *por medio* chord progression.

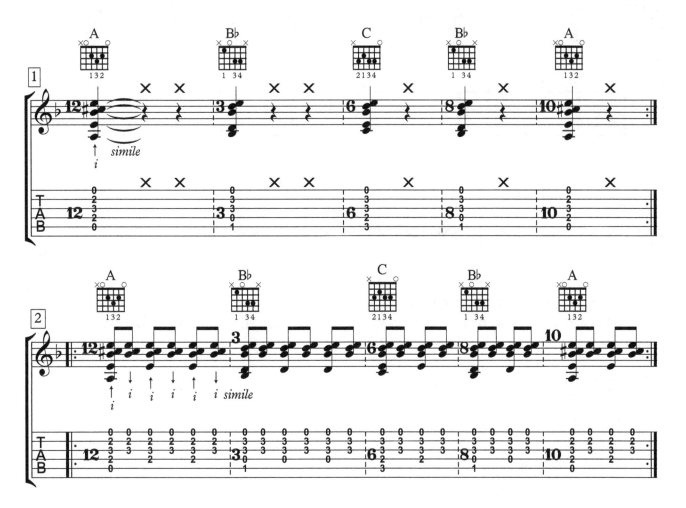

Feeling Compás on the Guitar (Cont.)

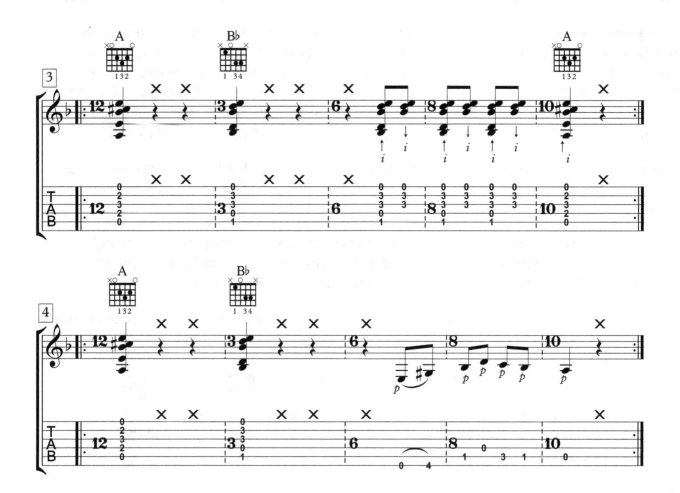

Once you are comfortable with these patterns, try alternating freely between all four.

Now that we have a basic understanding of how the 12-beat *compás* works, let's dive into the traditional starting place for flamenco guitarists, and the first lesson in our book: **Soleares**.

S oleares, or Soleá, is often called the "Mother of Flamenco" because it is the *palo* from which all of the other 12-beat forms are said to derive. The word Soleá itself is possibly derived from the Spanish word *soledad* or solitude, and it falls into the category of "*Cante Jondo*," a phrase meaning that it is deeply emotional. Viewed with great respect, and a certain reverence, flamenco singers and dancers tend to wait until they have mastered some of the lighter and faster *palos* before approaching Soleá. Yet guitarists typically begin their studies with Soleá because the slower tempo facilitates the acquisition of new guitar techniques.

A typical tempo range for Soleá is from around 50 beats per minute (BPM) to around 110 BPM. While Soleá is one of the most difficult forms to accompany, a solid understanding of Soleá helps us to grasp the compás, harmony, and melodic language of flamenco, therefore we will stick with tradition and also start our text with Soleá.

Basic Compás

The basic *compás* of Soleá is made up of two halves. The first half creates harmonic tension while the second half resolves it. The characteristic movement of the first half, is from an E-chord to an F-chord on the third beat, creating tension. The charactistic movement of the second half is to return to the E-chord on beat 10, resolving the tension.

Page four gives several typical variations for approaching the first half of the *compás*. Page five gives several common ways to return to beat 10. Musical phrases in Soleá will generally begin on beat 1 and lead into beat 3. Or, they will begin on beat 7 and lead into beat 10. Guitarists can then mix and match the two halves (see example 1), freely combining phrases from the first half of the rhythmic cycle with phrases from the second half. This creates dozens of potential variations of the basic 12-beat Soleá rhythm.

This concept of building individual *compases* out of component parts is one that you will use in all of the 12-beat forms. Because this concept is so important, take some extra time and get comfortable shuffling the two halves. We have illustrated one way of thinking about this with the example on page three.

You will notice that not every phrase begins exactly on beat 1 or 7, rather we have created variety by syncopating some of the beats. The syncopations in these examples are a quick way to broaden your rhythmic vocabulary. Syncopation plays an important role in contemporary flamenco.

There are two places in the rhythm to really watch out for:

- Don't rush through beats 4, 5, and 6. Though you may not be playing any notes during these beats, it is important to give them their full duration.

- You will also notice that there is a characteristic phrase that is played on beats 10 through 12, which helps to lead us into the next *compás*. This can be deceptively tricky, and this is a place where many students lose their sense of the rhythm.

Beats 7-10

Four options for "7 to 10" phrases

Beats 1-3

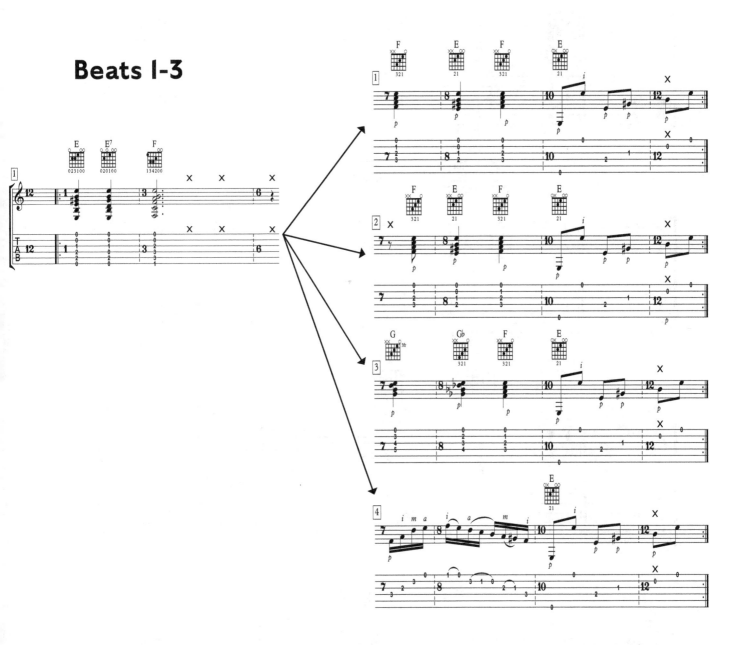

Soleá Basic Compás: First Half - Beats 1 to 6

Beat 1 leads to harmonic tension at beat 3.

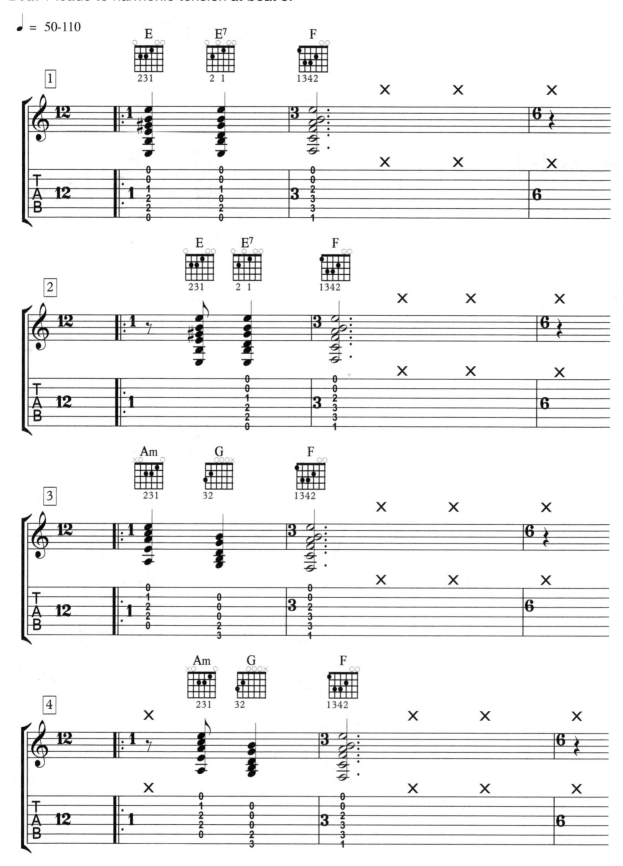

Soleá Basic Compás: Second Half - Beats 7 to 12

Beat 7 leads into a resolved harmony at beat 10.

Complete Compases

Here are some combinations of the first and second half of the Soleá *compás*, which together form some typical *compás* sequences. There is no need to play Soleá *compás* combinations in any particular order, but it is essential that you always incorporate both halves so that you create and resolve tension correctly with each *compás*.

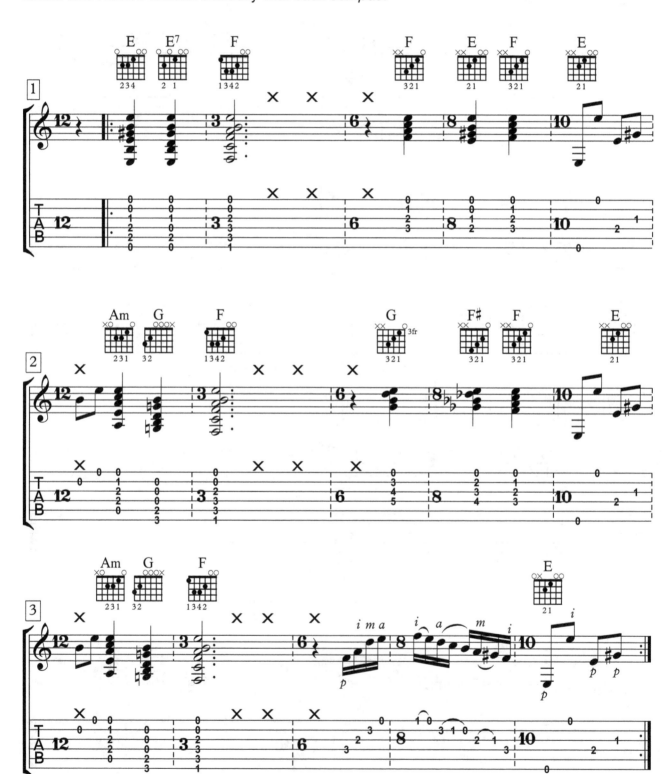

Escobilla Melodies

Eventually your basic *compás* will evolve to incorporate short melodic ideas, many of which will be derived from standard accompaniment patterns played in flamenco dance, specifically a section called the *escobilla*.

Almost all danced *palos* have an *escobilla* section that is designed to feature the dancer's rhythmic footwork. Therefore, one of the most important features of these melodies is a constant and clear pulse – you need to provide a solid beat for the dancer to dance to.

In Soleá, the *escobilla* is phrased a little differently than the regular *compás*: the divisions of the 12-beat cycle are felt in groups of three – **1** 2 3, **4** 5 6, **7** 8 9, **10** 11 12, rather than the more typical **12** 1 2, **3** 4 5, **6** 7, **8** 9, **10** 11. These *escobilla* melodies will always begin on the 1 of the 12-beat *compás* and are phrased in three-beat groups, much like any normal ¾ meter.

These melodies are used so often that the Soleá compás will feel like it is contantly shifting back-and-forth between a ¾ feel - strong three-beat groups - and the typical accents of the 12-beat cycle. At first these shifts might feel confusing, but they quickly become quite comfortable after some practice.

Simple Phrases

Here are some traditional, and very common, Soleá *escobilla* phrases that would fall under the rubric of playing *compás,* or keeping time. Over time, you will accumulate dozens of variations of these melodies, and they will help to form the basis of much of your *compás,* serving as "glue" to link larger sections of your Soleá.

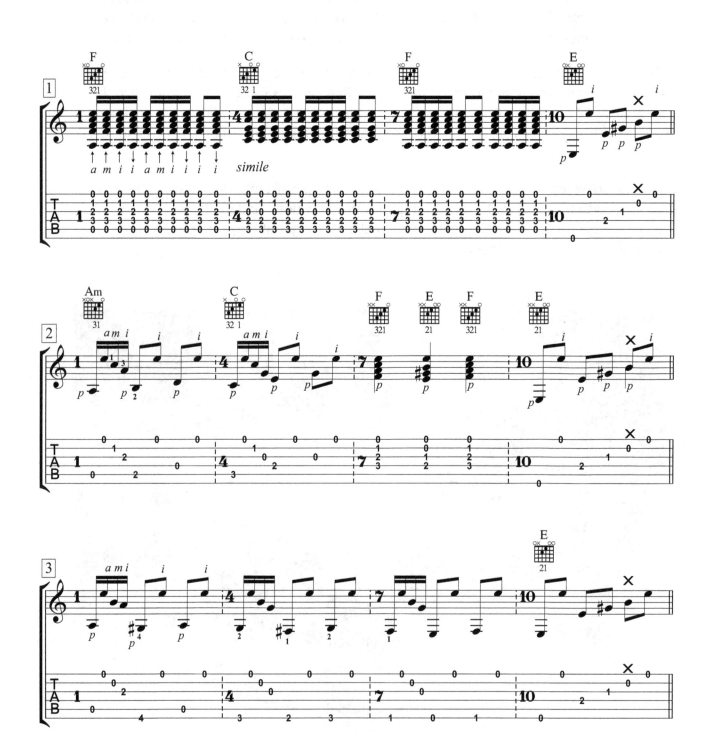

Escobilla: Phrase Variations

Escobilla: Two-Compás Phrases

Escobilla melodies will often be two *compases* long, allowing for phrases that are longer, and more harmonically varied. This variety is often achieved through quite subtle changes. In the two-*compás* example below, the only change from what you've seen previously is the addition of the note G on the first string in the second *compás*.

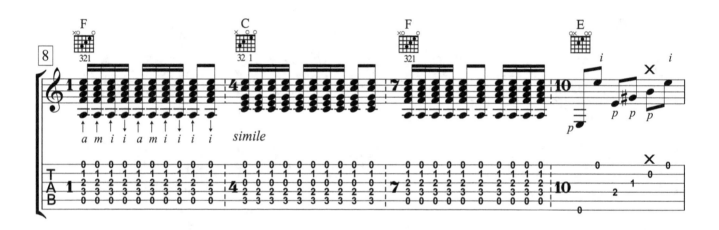

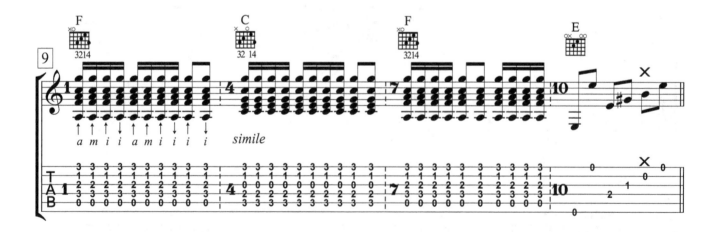

In other common two-*compás* melodies, variety is achieved by resolving to a secondary chord in the first *compás*, usually a G-chord (see *compás* 10). In the second *compás* of the pair, the music resolves normally, in this case back to the E-chord which we have come to expect. This works in other keys too, but the resolutions will go to different harmonies.

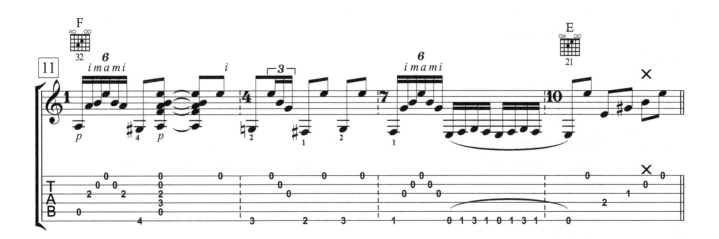

Falsetas

Using a Falseta as an Introduction (1.4-1.5)

The guitarist can begin the Soleá in several ways, the most traditional being a *llamada* (see page 20, *compás* 6), which is a simple statement of the basic *compás*. In more contemporary flamenco the introduction is often a *falseta* like the two introductions you find here. A *falseta* is a self-contained melodic idea, usually written by the guitarist.

Falseta (1.6)

This very traditional *falseta* addresses the use of the right-hand thumb. The development of a good thumb rest-stroke is one of the defining characteristics of flamenco technique and sound. For this reason it is very important to follow the *p-p-i-p* pattern in the right hand and not to replace it with *p-i-a-i* or some more 'comfortable' *arpeggio* pattern.

You will notice that like your escobilla melodies, most *falsetas* in Soleá begin on beat one and are phrased into groups of three beats. Don't be fooled! This is not simply a triple meter and is one reason Soleá can be deceptively difficult. Whoever you may be playing with will most likely be accenting within the typical twelve-beat pattern against your *falseta*.

Falseta (1.7)

This thumb-based *falseta* is another simple, traditional *falseta*. Be sure to take some care transitioning between the triplets of the *falseta* and the regular eighth notes of the cadences in beats 4 through 6 and beats 10 through 12.

Falseta (1.8)

This *falseta* frequently alternates between arpeggio (free-stroke) and *picado* (rest-stroke). The beginnings of the picado sections are marked with the * symbol. The picado sections should always alternate between i and m fingers. Generally the player can decide which finger, *i* or *m*, feels more comfortable to begin each passage with, but the long scale passage beginning on the ninth beat of the fourth *compás* must begin its *picado* alternation starting with *m* in order to avoid awkward string crossings later in the scale.

The *llamada* at the end of this falseta can be used to end the piece, or as a short introduction to the entire Soleá.

Falseta as Introduction

Notes: These introductory falsetas are most effective when the slurs in the left hand are crisp and clear, this also makes both Introduction 1 and 2 excellent left-hand workouts!

Intro (Soleá I.4)

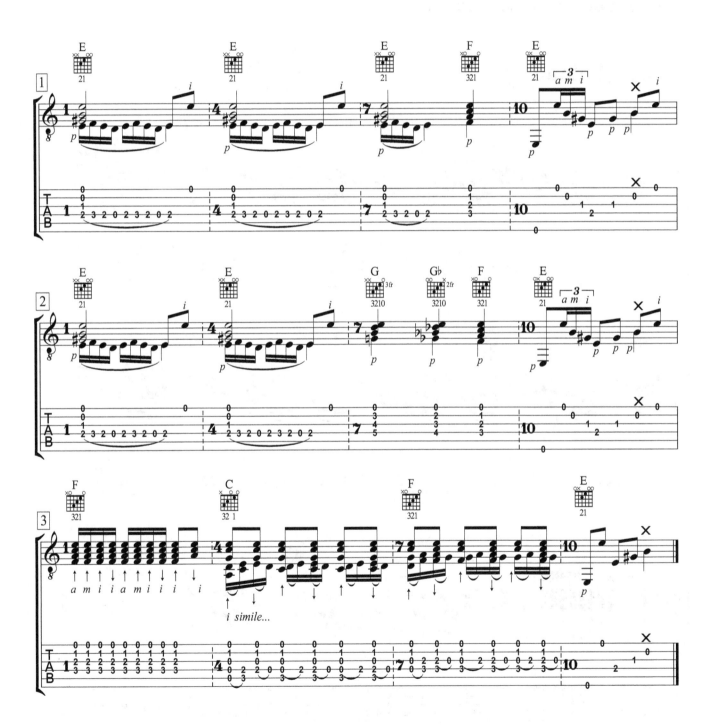

Falseta as Introduction: More Advanced

Notes: Introduction 1.5 is a more advanced variation of Introduction 1.4, so if Introduction 1.4 still feels challenging, you should hold off learning this *falseta* until you are ready.

The feathered beams in the second beat of compás 3 mean that this rasgueado steadily speeds up as it approaches the third beat.

Intro (Soleá 1.5)

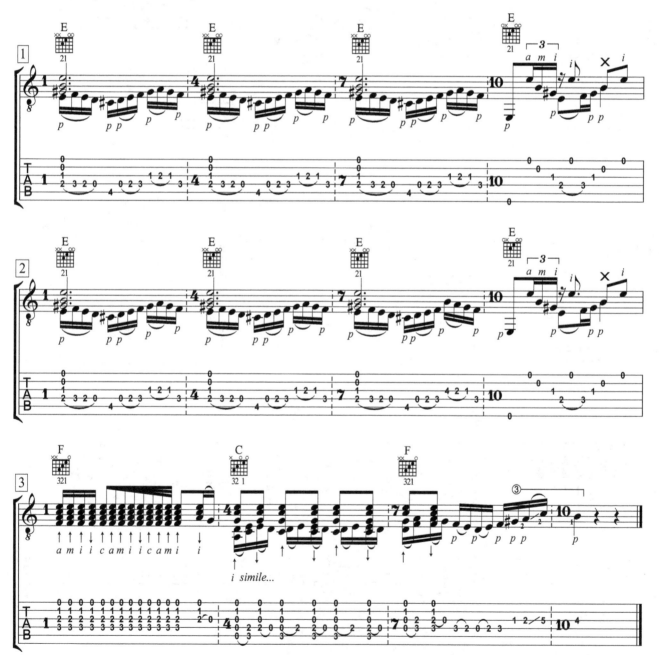

Falseta: Focussing on the Thumb

Notes: This *falseta* is a simple variant on one of the most traditional *falsetas* in Soleá.

Be sure that you are keeping a consistent beat as you transition between triplets and regular eighth notes. For instance, in *compás* 3, every three beats you will need to make one of these rhythmic shifts, between triplets and regular eighth notes. If you aren't sure if these transitions are happening rhythmically, this might be a good time to play along with a metronome.

- Do a true rest-stroke with the thumb every time you play, this means using the full weight of the right hand and forearm for every thumb stroke

- The point of this *falseta* is the thumb, so unless another finger is notated, use your thumb for everything!

Falseta (Soleá 1.6)

Falseta: Arpeggio with Thumb and Index

Notes: This very traditional *falseta* again addresses the use of the right-hand thumb, for this reason it is very important to follow the *p-p-i-p* pattern in the right hand.

- Again, use the full weight of the right hand and forearm on every thumb rest-stroke

- Don't worry if the right-hand thumb and index finger bump into one another, this is a natural occurrence and will not affect the sound

- The point of this *falseta* is the thumb, so be sure to follow the right-hand fingering closely

Falseta (Soleá 1.7)

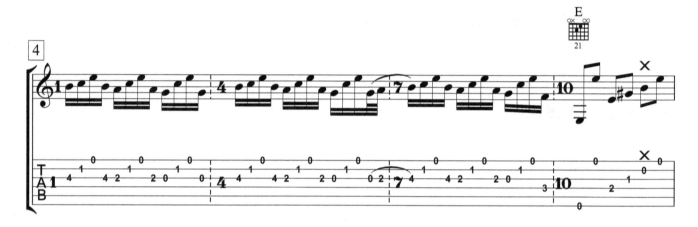

Falseta: Arpeggio-Picado Alternation

Notes: Strive for a smooth transition from arpeggio to picado with minimal change in right-hand position

In the longer scale section beginning on the tenth beat of the fourth *compás*, use the accents on 10, 12, 3, and 6 to help you organize the scale in time, and most importantly, to help you keep your awareness of your place within the 12-beat cycle.

Each "measure" involves a change of chord, be sure to connect the last note of each scale passage to the first note of each thumb passage. For instance, the last note of beat 3 to the first note of beat 4.

Falseta (Soleá I.8)

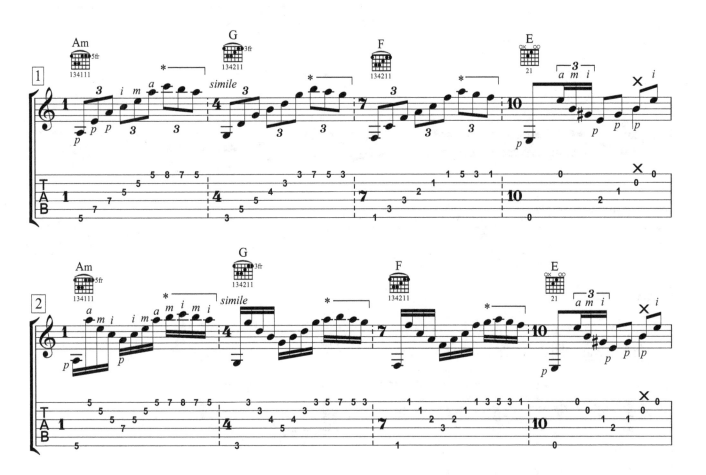

(Llamada)

Soleá: Constructing a Solo

Now that you have the musical tools for playing Soleá, you can put them to use in a variety of ways. You can be creative in how you stucture your Soleá, and you will want to change the format depending on whether you are playing solo guitar, with *cante*, or with both *cante* and *baile*. The chart below represents the format for a traditional Soleá guitar solo.

It should be noted that the singer is every bit as important as the guitarist for dance accompaniment, therefore you are very unlikely to see a true flamenco dance performance without cante.

(Pick any of these)
- Llamada
- Intro Falseta
- Any other Falseta

Always connect your ideas with Compás, it's the glue!

(Pick any of these)
- Falseta 1, 2, or 3
- Any other Soleá Falseta por arriba

This can be identical to your previous compás, or something brand new, it's up to you.

- Falseta 1, 2, or 3
- Avoid using the same Falseta twice
- Any other Soleá Falseta por arriba

This can be identical to your previous compás, or something brand new, it's up to you.

- Subida
- Llamada, or any Falseta that culminates in a llamada
- Any Compás phrase where stopping on beat ten is logical
- Either "Intro" Falseta ending on beat ten also work great as endings

Chapter 2 • Tangos

FLAMENCO EXPLAINED

At this point you may be relieved to learn that Tangos, our next *palo*, is in good old-fashioned $\frac{4}{4}$ time, which should come more naturally to most guitarists. While it is in a regular quadruple meter, one of the characteristic features of Tangos *compás* is the absence of a strong downbeat. In other words, we often avoid playing on beat one. It should also be noted that Tangos is not often danced with the same kind of complex structure that the Soleá has, and later Alegrías will have too - rather it is typically danced *por fiesta*.

Tangos, Rumbas, and Bulerías can all be danced *por fiesta*. This means that a variety of dancers, singers, and musicians will share the stage, with each dancer performing a short burst of footwork called a *patada* (usually pronounced "*Patá*" in Spain). During each *patada* a singer will sing a *letra* of Tangos, Rumba, or Bulerías, as the case may be, and the dancer will dance in response to the *cante*, and then close the *patada* with a small flourish. This is different than a dance solo in that there is generally none of the buildup or complexity we see in Alegrías or Soleá.

(Occasionally, novice dancers will want to insert long sections of footwork they have learned in dance class during a patada. While this is not really in the spirit of por fiesta, just run with it if it happens).

Often, Tangos will also appear as the *macho*, or last section, of a Tientos. (Rumba is in turn the *macho* of the Tangos). Similar to *palos* that use the 12-beat cycle, four-beat *palos* also tend to build in speed and intensity as the piece progresses. The *palos* in order of tempo can be grouped as follows: Tientos (slow), Tangos (medium), Rumba (fast). A typical tempo range for Tangos is from around 90 BPM to around 180 BPM. Since we will have a slightly easier time with *compás* in Tangos, we'll use this opportunity to explore some new techniques and play some slightly more challenging *falsetas*.

Basic Compás: Two-Measure Phrases

Notes: Even though the Tangos *compás* is in a more standard $\frac{4}{4}$ meter, it is often grouped into two or four-measure groups. Like Soleá, we can mix and match the first and second half of our phrases - and generally this works with both two-measure and/or four-measure phrases.

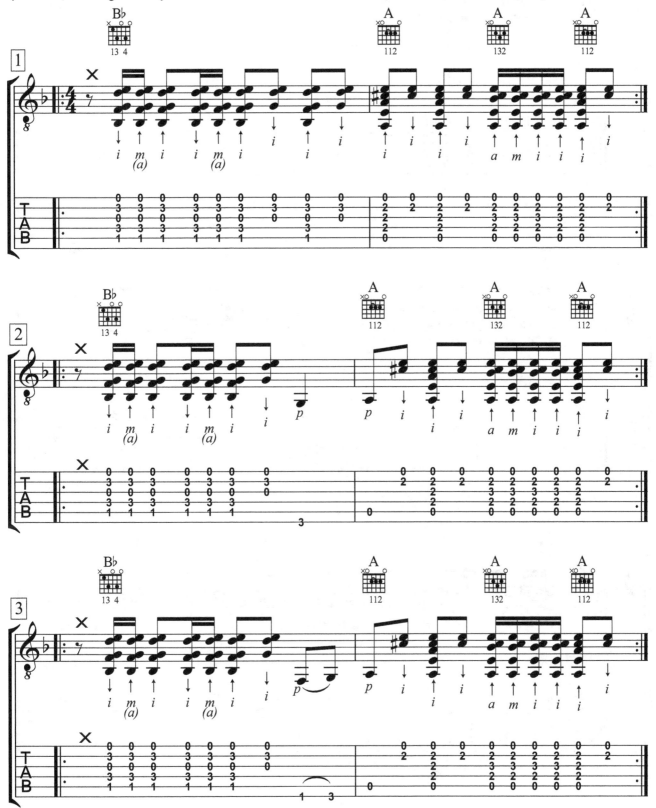

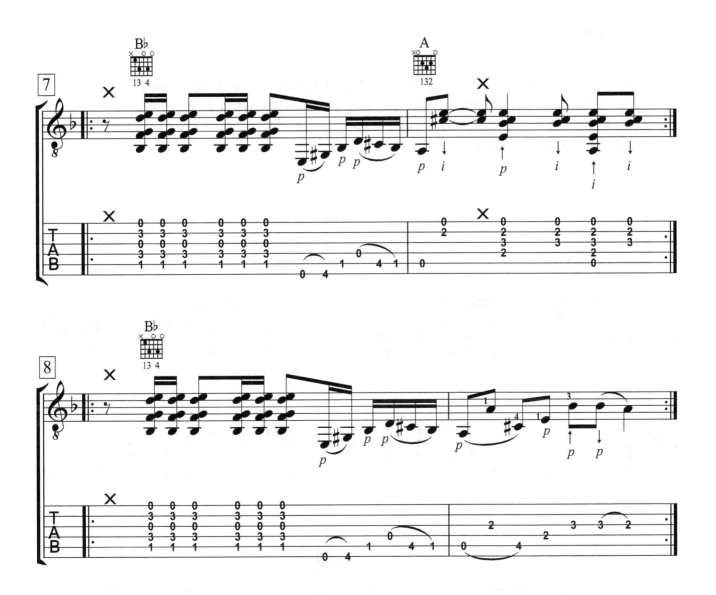

Basic Compás: Four-Measure Phrases

Here are some common four-measure phrases. You may notice that the third and fourth bars are based on the two-measure basic *compás* units. Feel free to mix and match the second half of these four-measure phrases with any of the two-measure basic *compás* patterns from that section (2.1).

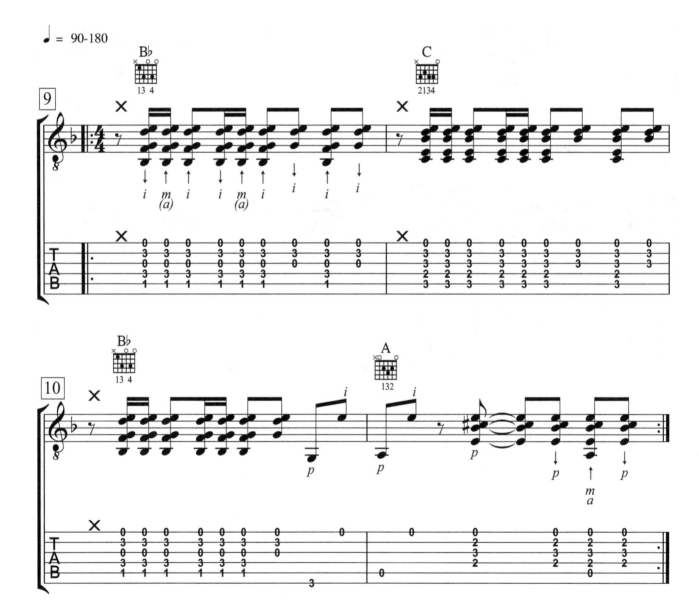

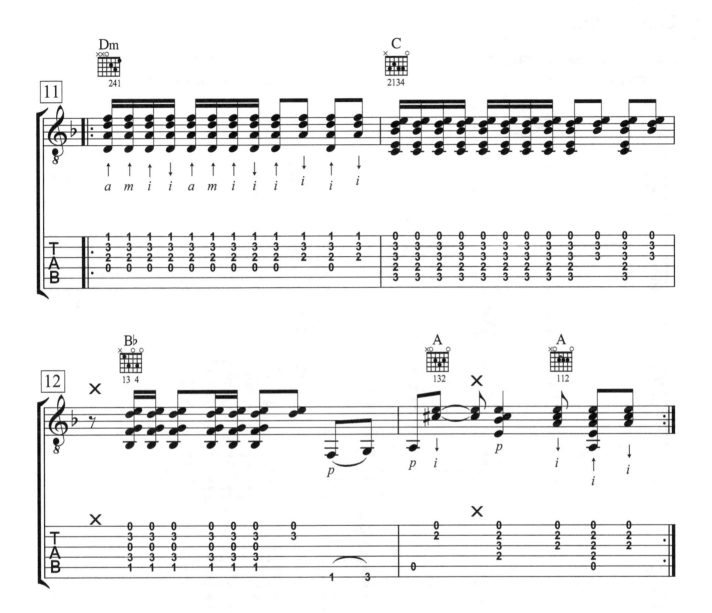

Llamadas

Llamadas in Tangos tend to stress the "don't play on one" feeling of the Tangos, and as a general rule either stick to quarter notes on beats 2, 3, and 4, or have triplets on those three beats.

There are many two- and four-measure *llamadas*. The four-measure variety often incorporates a common two-measure *llamada* into its second half.

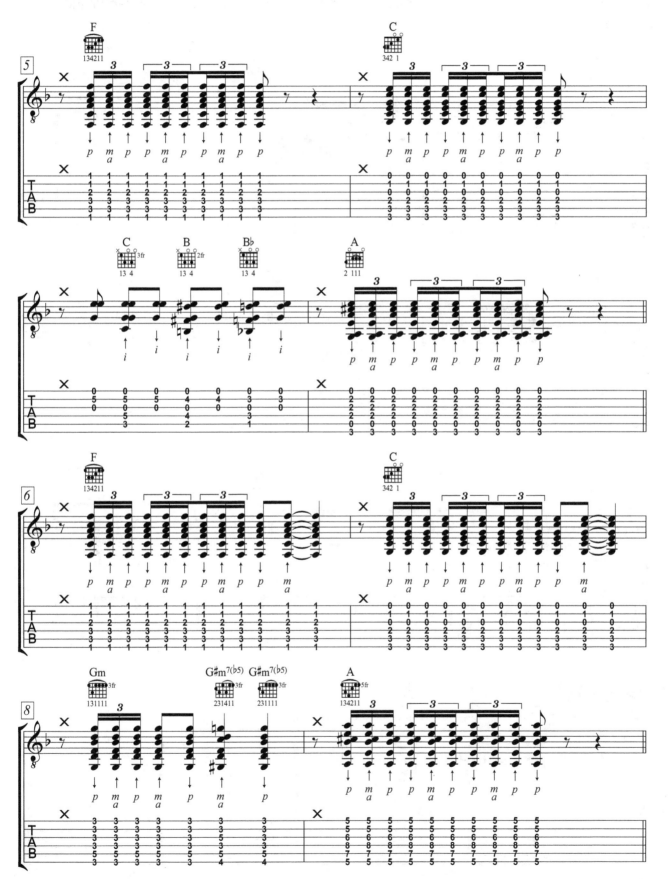

Falseta (2.4): Alzapua

Before beginning this *falseta* it might be a good time to review flamenco thumb technique on page 135.

Falseta (2.5): More Advanced

Once you are comfortable with the chord voicings, this is not an overly demanding *falseta*. Make sure you understand the rhythms, sing the melody if possible, and go for a strong, warm tone with the right-hand thumb. Playing this *falseta* slowly with a metronome, and being true to the rhythms, will result in a better understanding of the Tangos feel.

(Llamada continued)

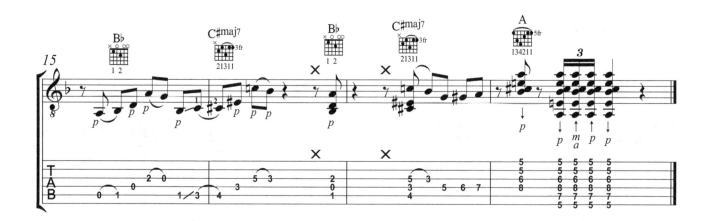

Falseta (2.6): Combining Arpeggio, Picado, and Alzapua

This *falseta* incorporates three of the major right-hand techniques - arpeggio, *picado*, and *alzapua* - and also has some serious syncopation to contend with. As always, make sure you understand the rhythms you are playing first, and then learn each section until you feel the *compás* and know where to come in. We can break this *falseta* down into eight *compases* of arpeggio, four *compases* of *picado*, four *compases* of *alzapua,* and a two-*compás* closure. A good approach might be to learn each section individually, and then connect them when you feel ready.

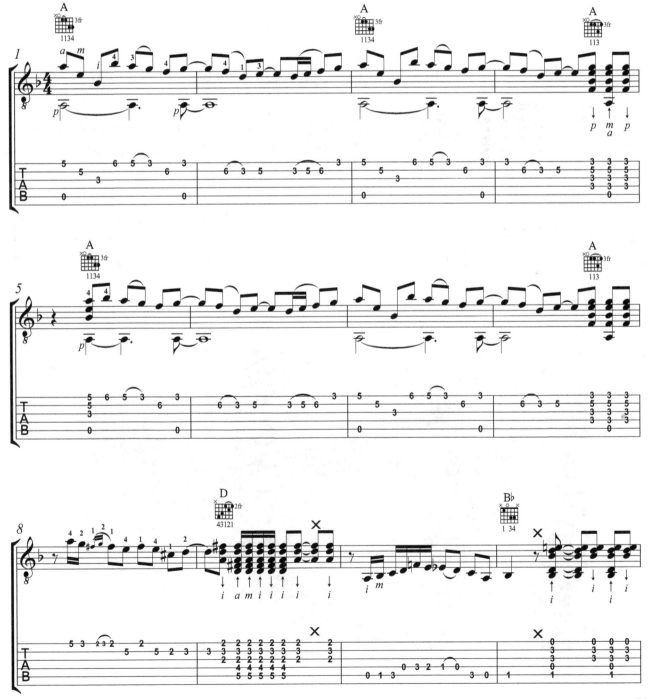

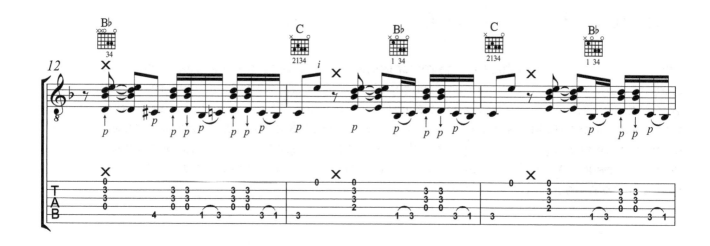

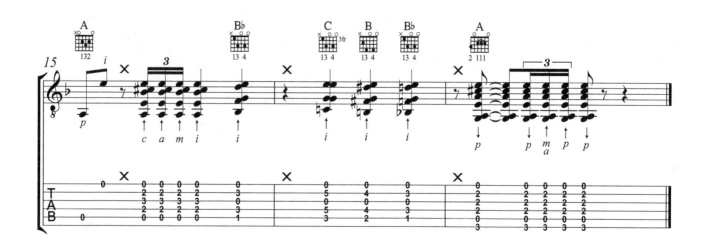

Tangos: Constructing a Solo

As you saw in Soleá, you can now use the material you've learned in a variety of ways. You can be creative in how you stucture your Tangos, and you will want to change the format depending on whether you are playing solo guitar, with *cante*, or with both *cante* and *baile*. The chart below will get you started in constructing a solo guitar Tangos.

(Pick any of these)
- Intro Falseta
- Llamada
- Any other Falseta
- Tapado compás is also a nice way to set your groove

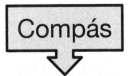

As you use llamadas to punctuate your compás and falsetas, remember to alternate between shorter 2-measure, and longer 4-measure, llamadas.

You can use one of your less-intense llamadas to introduce a falseta. Remember, llamadas are not only used as exclamation points, but can also be great commas and periods.

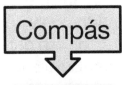

Another note on llamadas, you don't need to play a llamada every time you transition between falsetas. Also, you can use a softer dynamic on the same llamada to create variety.

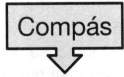

The bulk of a Solo Tangos is stringing together your falsetas in an artful way. Remember to simply enjoy the groove of basic compás.

End on 3!

*If you hear someone's Tangos end on beat 1, don't worry, it's OK, there's a reason for that. However, that reason is beyond the scope of this book.

Sevillanas are a little different from all of the other *palos*. To begin with, it is among the group of *palos* called *aflamencados* (a form, not of gypsy origin, that has been adapted and incorporated into the flamenco tradition). Sevillanas has its origins in traditional Spanish dance. Sevillanas are popular throughout Spain and are most often seen as a couple's dance, which is probably why it has become so widespread in the Spanish general populace. It is one of the few social dances in flamenco and the only flamenco *palo* to have a fixed structure. In the *tablao* setting, and in general, Sevillanas are sung, but there are also many great solo-guitar Sevillanas that range from simple to virtuosic. All Sevillanas share a common structure and length. A typical tempo range for Sevillanas is from around 100 BPM to around 200 BPM. Sevillanas are in a $\frac{3}{4}$ meter but like all flamenco, you can expect a great deal of syncopation.

One Sevillanas is really four short dances strung together, each of which is also referred to as a Sevillana. You may find that the exact same music is repeated all four times, or four separate short pieces may be strung together. The dance steps tend to change with each Sevillana, but you as the guitarist do not necessarily need to change anything, since the overall rhythm and structure are identical. Instrumental versions, however, will tend to use different music for each component Sevillana in order to add variety. As in our example, four distinct melodies in four separate keys is the norm.

Sevillanas: Three Main Sections

Each component Sevillana will adhere to the following three sections. Although, not everyone names them in the same way. Therefore, we will simply label them as follows:

I. Introduction

Sometimes called the *entrada*, this introduction is the one section of the form that can vary in length. It generally consists of the musicians keeping time until the singer enters with the *salida*. Its flexible length allows for the musicians to wait until all the dancers have found a partner, and are ready to begin. In Kai's Sevillanas, the introduction is always 12 measures long.

2. The Salida

The *salida* usually consists of a shortened section of the main melody, either sung or played, in order to let the dancers know that the danced portion of the form is about to begin. This is always three measures long.

3. The Copla

The main section of the Sevillana is the *copla* (verse), though you may also hear the word *copla* used to refer to an entire Sevillana. It is twelve measures long and is always repeated three times. Often when Sevillanas are sung, the first two coplas are identical while the third is a variation. Similarly, some solo-guitar Sevillanas will also vary the third repetition of the *copla* like we do here.

The name Kai gave to this Sevillanas is Marchena. The title is in homage to the guitarist Enrique de Melchor, whose father was the great guitarist Melchor de Marchena. Marchena is a pueblo on the outskirts of Sevilla. The particular groove of these Sevillanas is drawn from the groove that Enrique de Melchor taught him and used in his own piece titled Huele a Romero.

Solo Guitar Sevillana No. 1

Intro

Salida

Coplas 1-2

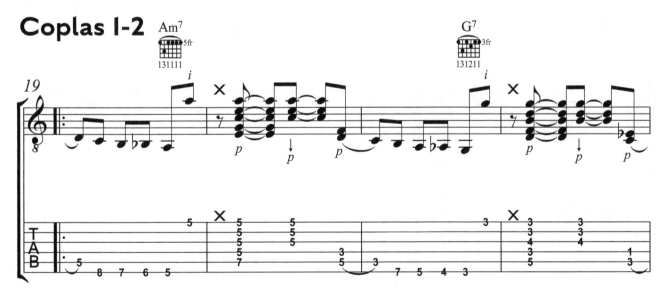

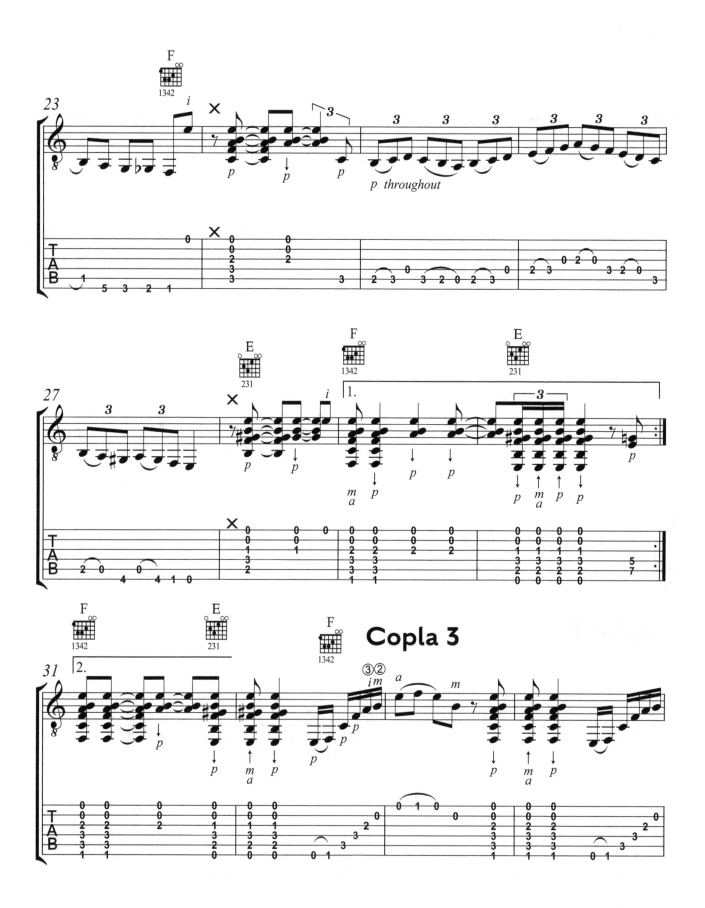

Solo Guitar Sevillana No. 2

Intro

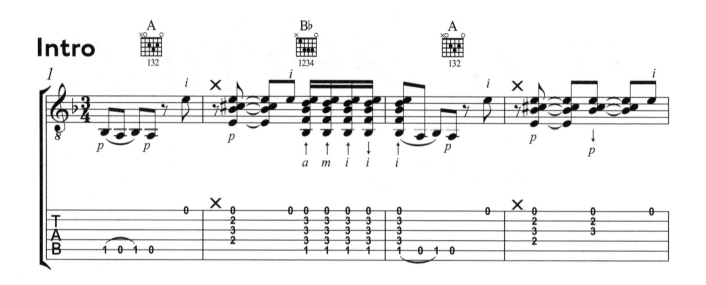

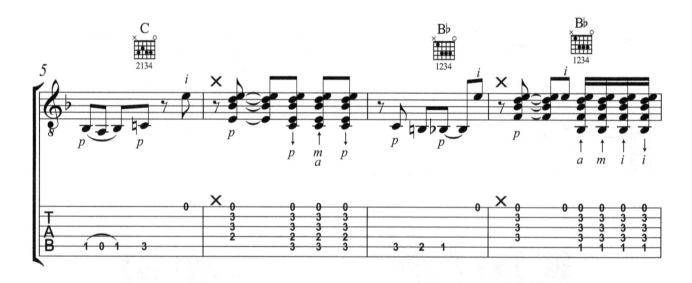

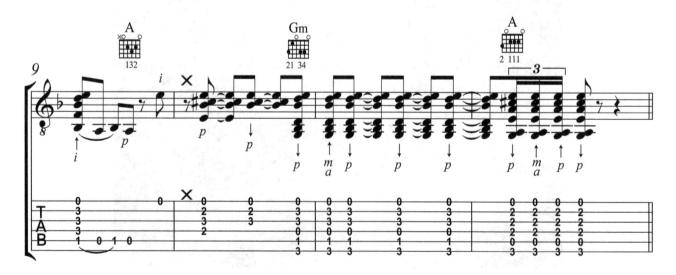

Salida

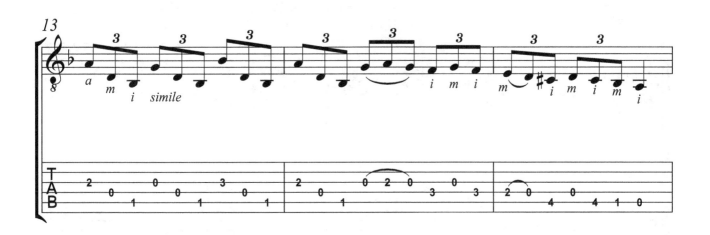

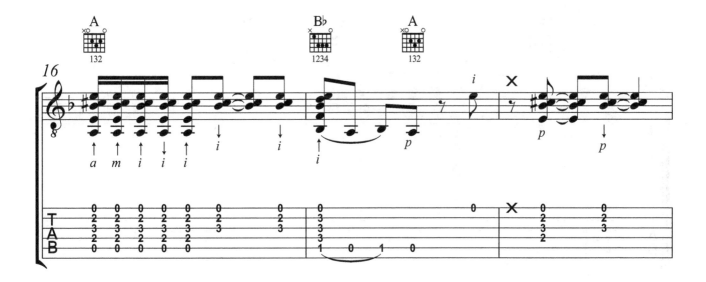

Coplas I-2

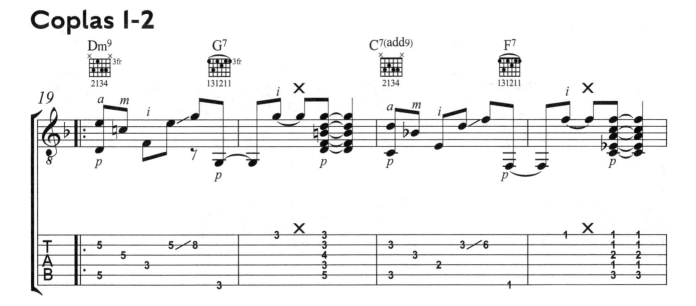

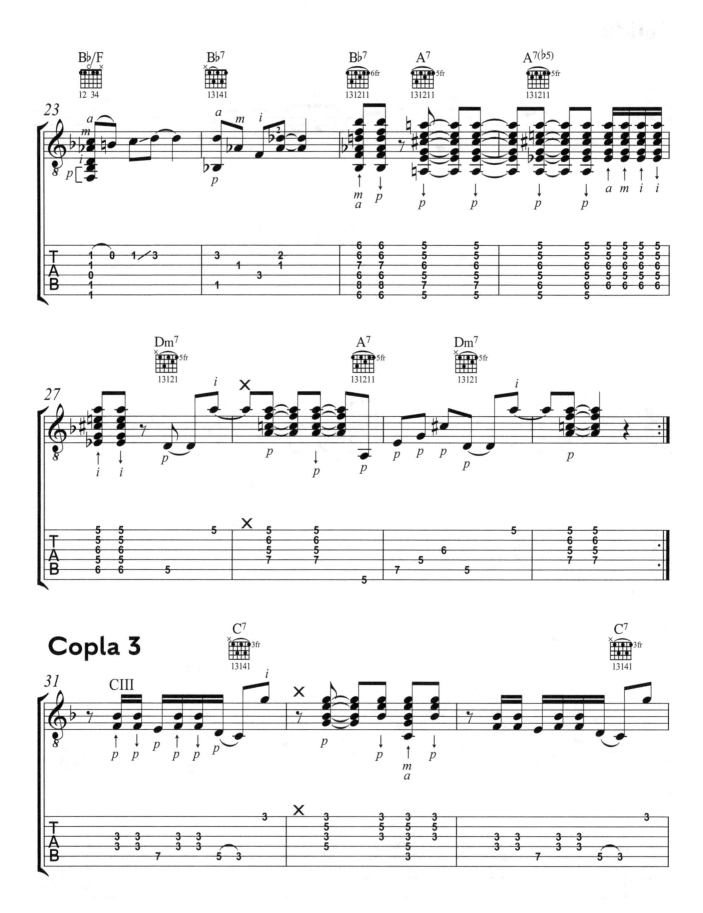

Solo Guitar Sevillana No. 3

Intro

Salida

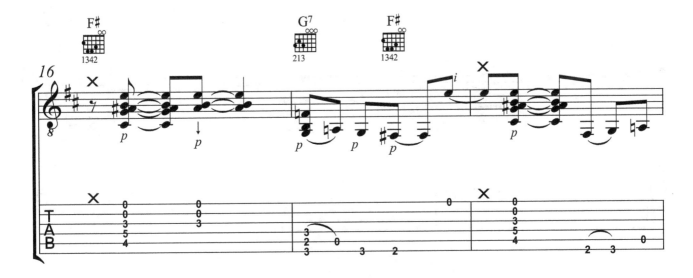

Coplas 1-2

Copla 3

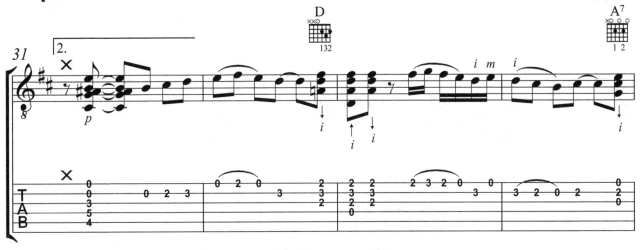

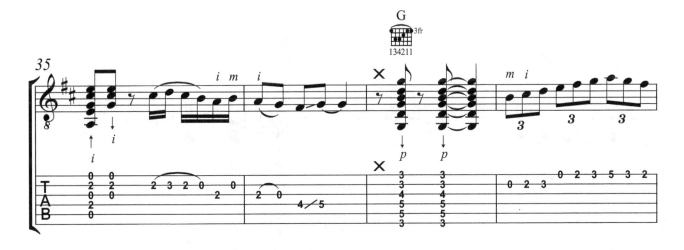

Solo Guitar Sevillana No. 4

Intro

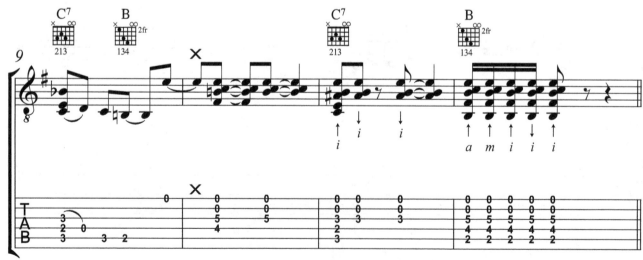

Salida

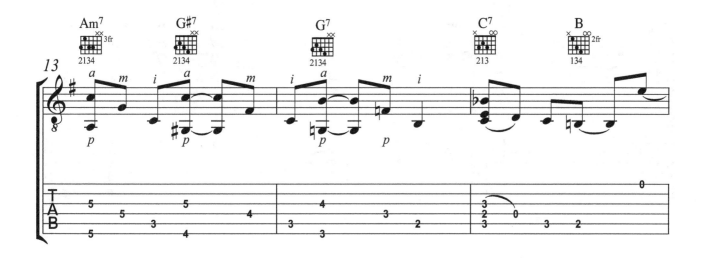

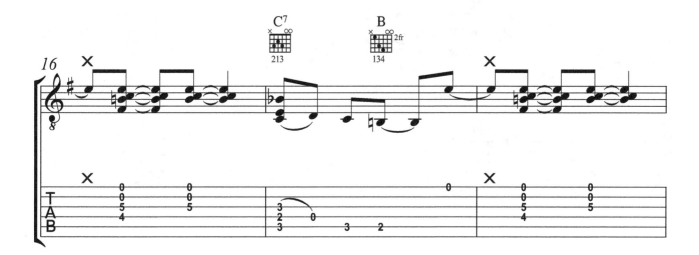

Coplas I-2

Copla 3

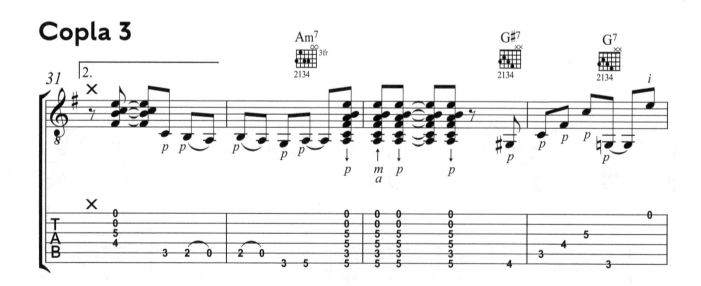

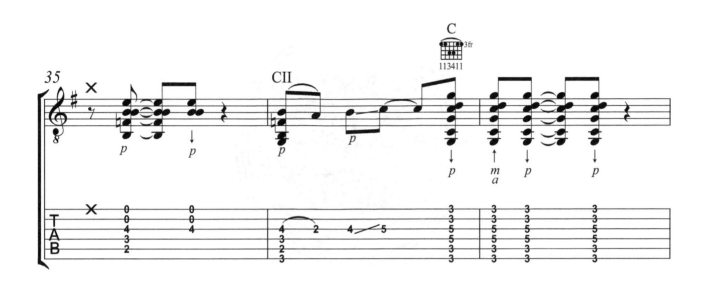

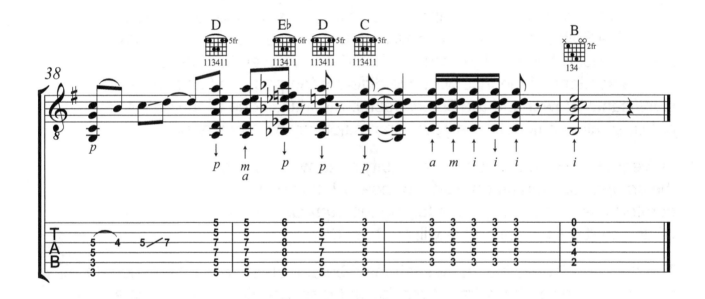

Chapter 4 • Alegrías

FLAMENCO
EXPLAINED

Alegrías is a *palo* that originated in the port city of Cadiz, and many of the *letras* are about sailors and sailing. The *compás* is a 12-beat cycle, like Soleá, but generally faster. A typical tempo range for Alegrías is from around 100 BPM to around 180 BPM. However, the *Silencio* and Bulería sections of Alegrías will have different tempos, the *Silencio* being significantly slower and the Bulería faster. Alegrías is one of the major-key *palos*, so all traditional rules governing major-key harmony apply.

In Alegrías we also encounter ambiguity as to whether we should think of the *compás* as starting on beat 1 or beat 12. It is best to simply become comfortable with both ways of feeling the *compás*, as some phrases will clearly start on 1 while others will start on 12.

The danced Alegrías has more sections than any other *palo* in flamenco. In addition to the *salidas*, *letras*, *llamadas*, *subidas*, and Bulerías that we see in Soleá, an Alegria has two sections that are unique to it: the *Silencio* and the *Castellana*. While there is no absolute order to the sequence of sections in Alegrías, there are some general things we can expect.

While Alegrías is most traditionally played in the key of E major on the guitar, the keys of C and A are also common, and really any major key can be used as long as it is within the singer's range.

Basic Compás

On paper Soleá and Alegrías are very similar. The main difference is that Alegrías is played in a major key and at a significantly faster tempo. Like Soleá's harmonic movement, going from an E-chord to an F-chord and then back to E, in Alegrías we move from E to B7 on beat 3, and resolve back to E on beat 10. Also like Soleá, we can derive an incredible amount of variation in each *compás* by intermixing our phrases that lead from beat 12 (or 1) into beat 3, and our phrases that lead from beat 6 (or 7) into beat 10.

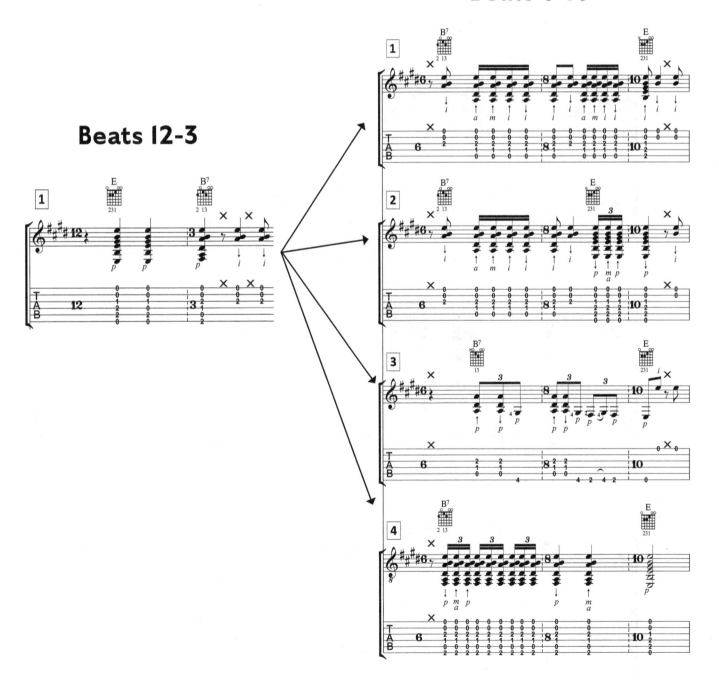

Beats 6-10

Beats 12-3

Alegrías Basic Compás: First Half - Beats 12 to 5

Beats 1 or 12 lead to harmonic tension at beat 3.

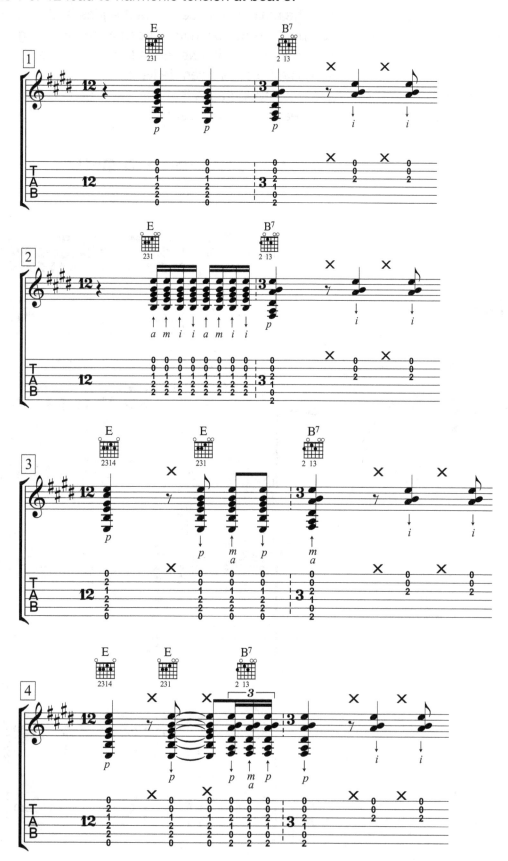

Alegrías Basic Compás: Second Half - Beats 6 to 12

Beats 6 or 7 lead into a resolved harmony at beat 10.

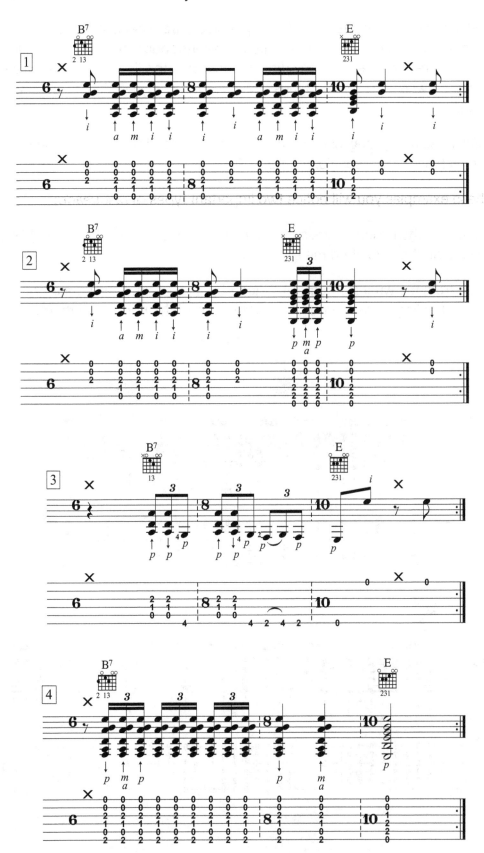

Llamadas

As discussed in the Glossary, the *llamada* will punctuate transitions between sections of a dance, or changes in musical phrase, such as an introduction into a *falseta*. In Alegrías, where there are often so many differing sections, the *llamada* is essential for the communication between dancers and musicians. Almost every section of Alegrías will end with a *llamada*.

These four *llamadas* are typical, single-*compás,* statements of the Alegrías tonality and rhythm, each with a strong resolution on beat 10.

Notes: In these examples you will notice two important types of *rasgueado*:

1. *Rasgueado* with the fingers - flicking from the hand requires us to fix the right-hand thumb with a bent first joint on the sixth string.

2. *Rasgueado* from the wrist (sometimes called Abanico) - Motion is initiated by the wrist and involves the fingers as a group, and both sides of the right-hand thumbnail.

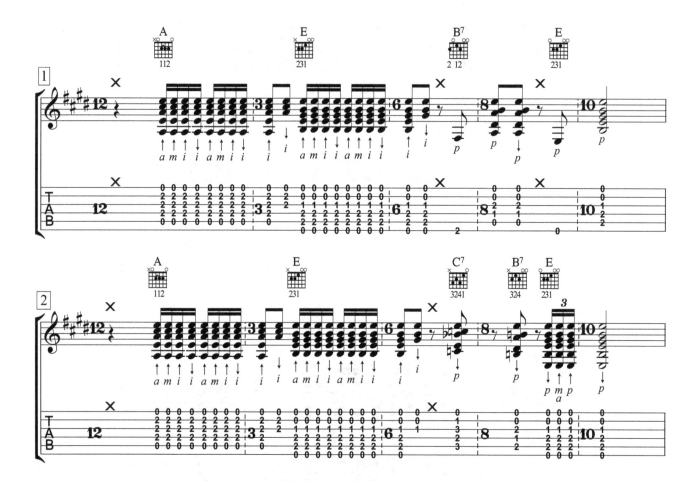

Llamadas: More Advanced

Since the free, wrist-based *rasgueado* is the strongest, these *llamadas* may be most appropriate at the loudest and most intense moments of the piece. Even though there are lots of notes, these can be played very fast once you get the hang of it! But, be sure to practice them slowly and evenly - the more you practice at a slow tempo with rhythmic precision, the better.

Notes: In beats 7 and 8 of the fourth *llamada* you will see a new kind of *golpe* (see *FlamencoExplained.com* for a video demonstration). This *golpe* is executed by hitting the guitar before contacting the sixth string as part of the downstroke with *i*.

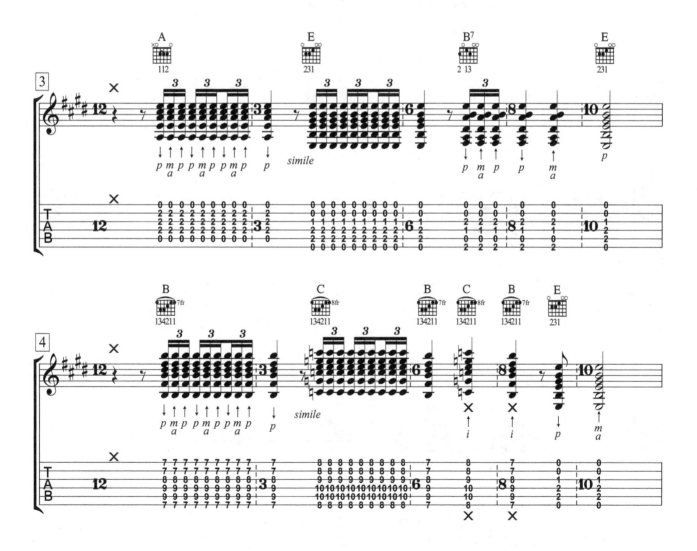

Falsetas in Alegrías

Falseta as Introduction

Like Soleá, Alegrías often begins with the guitarist playing *compás*. In more contemporary flamenco the introduction is often a *falseta*. This *falseta* serves well as an introduction and concludes with a *llamada* (the fifth *compás*) to signal that the *falseta* is complete and the piece can then move on to the next section with the addition of *cante* or *baile*.

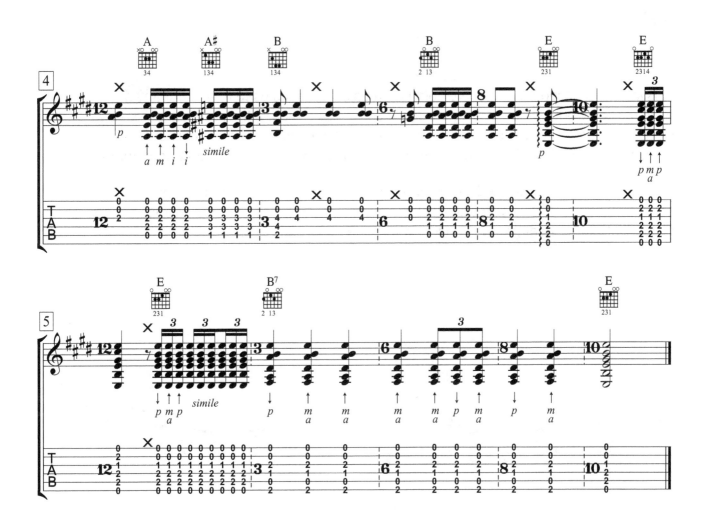

Falseta: Escobilla Phrase

This *falseta* is based on one of the common musical phrases used to accompany a dancer's heelwork section in Alegrías called *escobilla*. Typically, the *escobilla* phrases will be arranged in a two-*compás* pattern that, unlike usual *compás*, waits until beat 10 to move from chords E to B7, then resolves back to E on beat 10 in the following *compás*.

As in Soleá, the guitarist needs to provide a clear pulse for the dancer to follow, so this solo version is a great way to practice keeping a very steady pace. The melodies are again divided into three-beat groups and you will notice that each *compás* begins on beat 1.

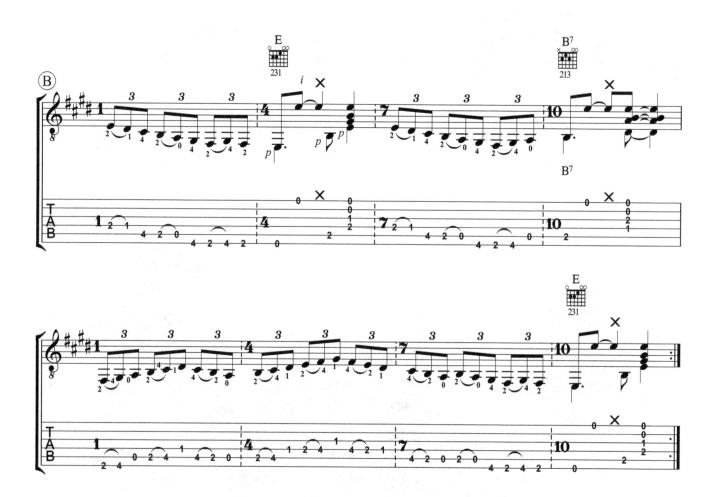

Falseta: A New Golpe

In this *falseta* we use a percussive slap with the palm of our right hand that is actually a type of *golpe*. In the notation, this will appear as follows: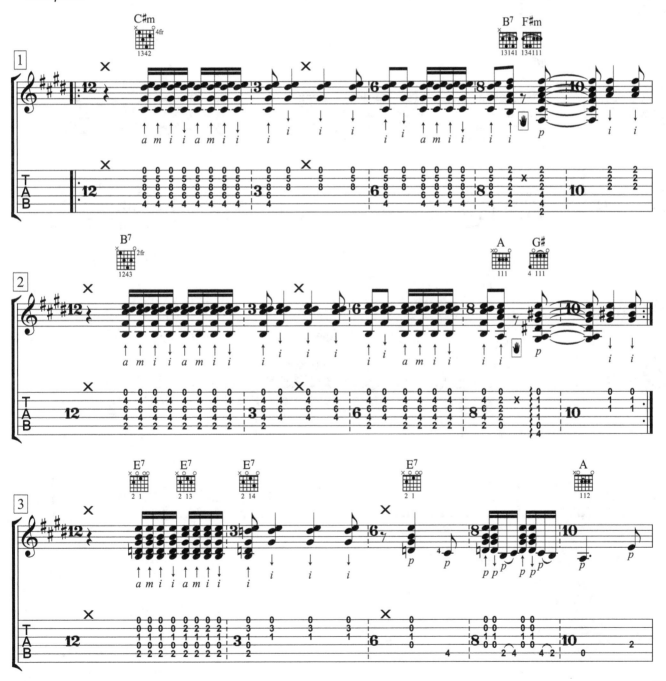

To achieve this, we slap all six strings with the open right hand, with the effect of simultaneously muting the strings and making the slapping sound. Following this *golpe*, we typically strum down with the flesh of the thumb. Often, the slap will occur on the downbeat and the downward strum will occur after the beat, on the "and" of the beat, creating a syncopation. The first time this occurs in this falseta is on beat 9 of the first *compás*.

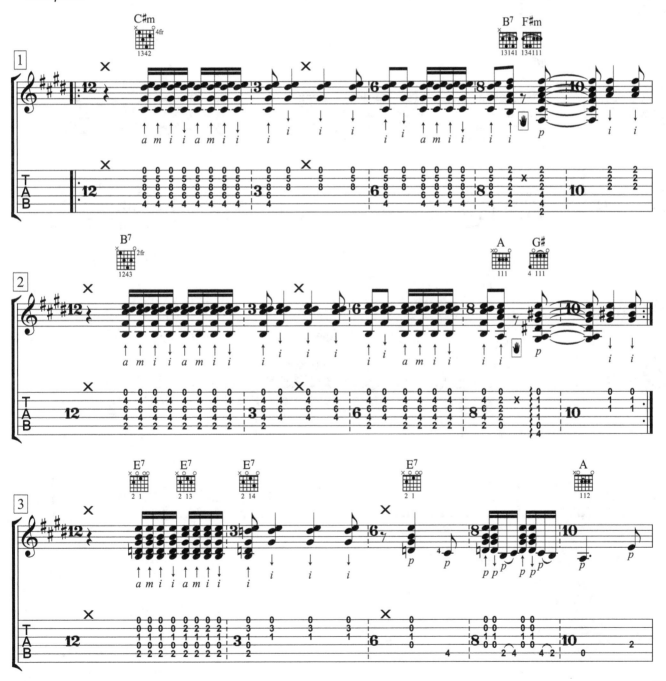

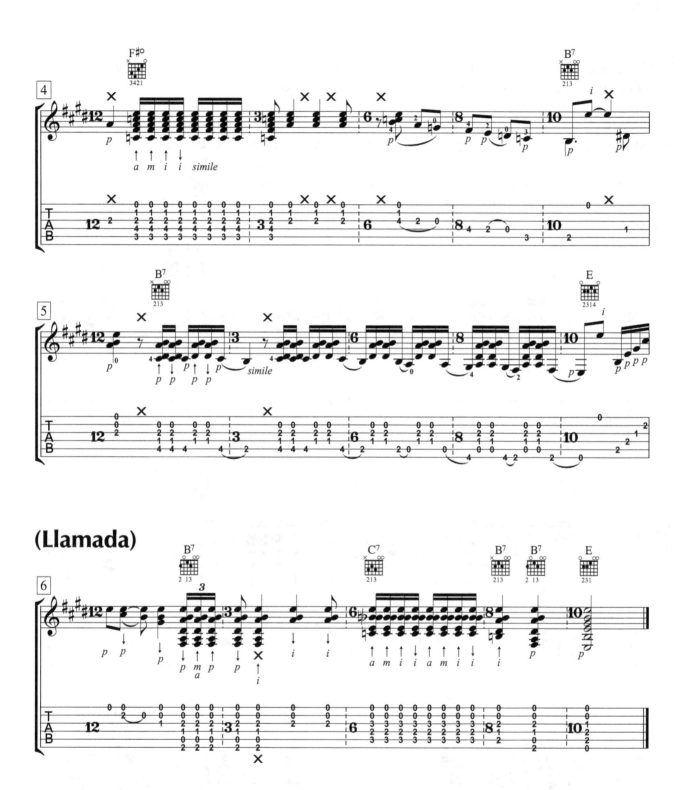

(Llamada)

Falseta: More Advanced

The scales in this *falseta* are short little bursts of sixteenth notes followed by slower triplets. These shouldn't be very difficult as long as you prepare them well. It is best to begin the first and third scale (first *compás* at beat 6, and third *compás* at beat 6) with your *i* finger and the second (second *compás* at beat 6) with your *m* finger. Take the time to be very aware of each string crossing after beginning with the correct right-hand finger. This will make the sometimes difficult transitions between strings smoother and easier, and therefore faster.

Because the scales start off-the-beat, on the "and" of beat 6, make sure you feel the first two sixteenth notes as pickups into beat 7. If we accent the first note of the scales too much, we can confuse the rhythm for ourselves, and anyone else with whom we are playing.

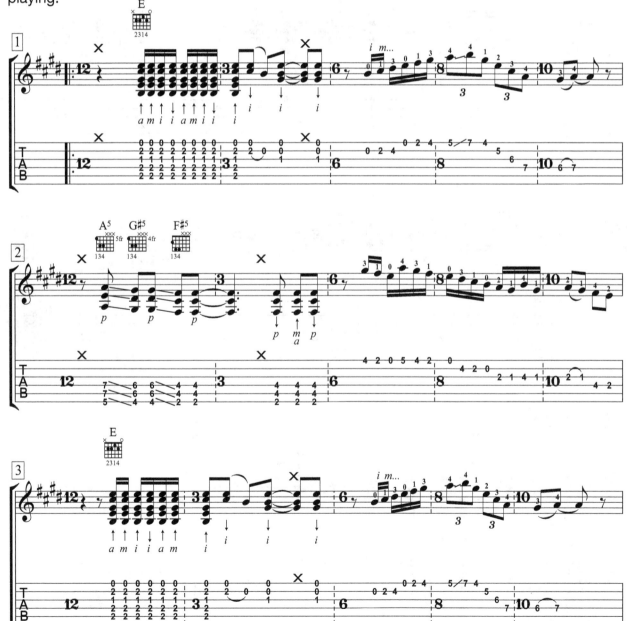

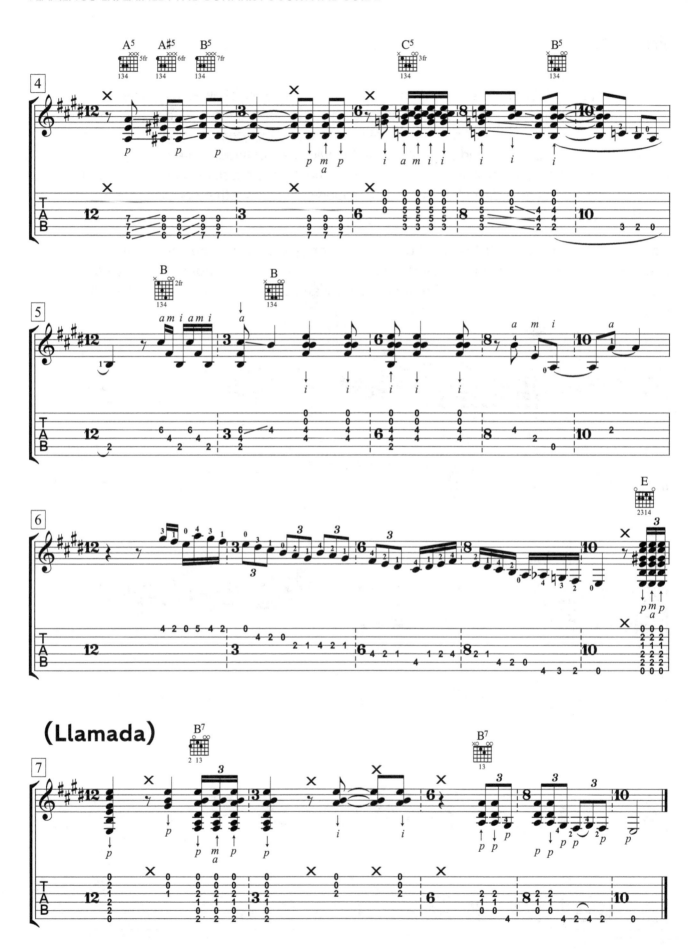

(Llamada)

Falseta: Silencio

The *silencio* is a lyrical section of the dance that has also inspired some lovely musical phrases on the guitar. A typical *silencio* is in the parallel minor key from the rest of the Alegrías, in this case E-minor from E-major. They are almost always six *compases* long, and significantly slower, and more free, than the other sections of the Alegría. It can be played strictly in *compás* with palmas, or more rubato without. Similar to *escobilla*, the phrasing is in two-*compás* sections that are phrased in three-beat groups. You will notice that the harmonies tend to change on beat 10.

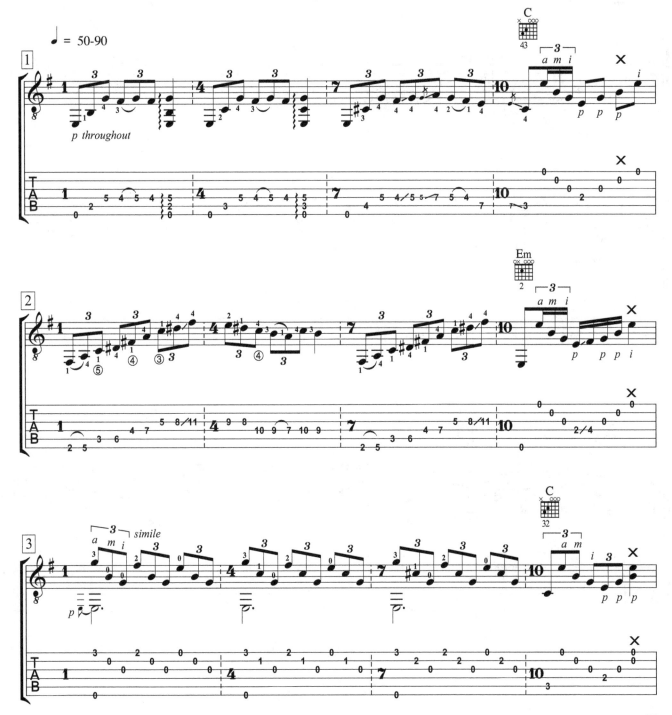

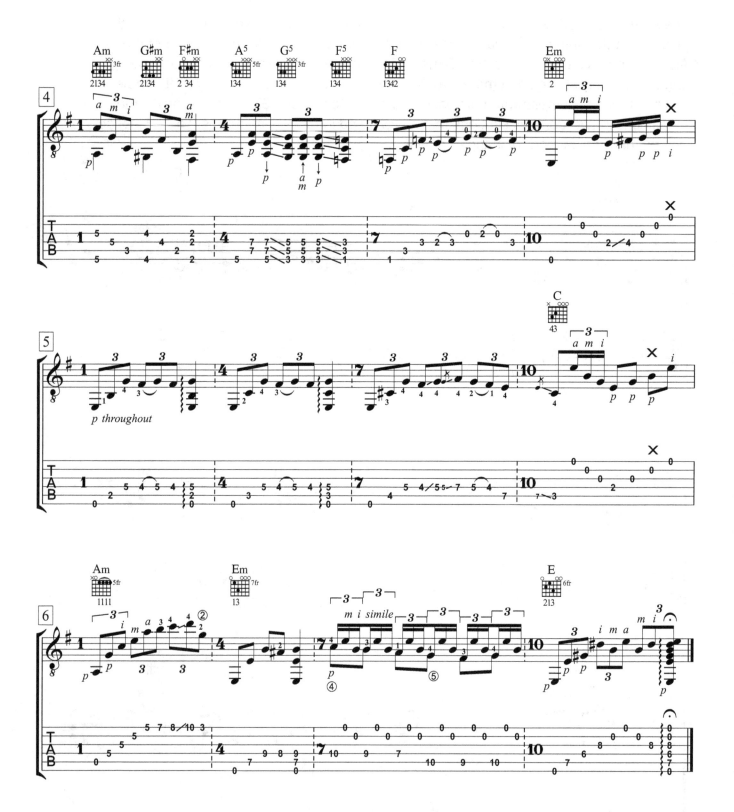

Alegrías: Constructing a Solo

(Pick any of these)
- Intro Falseta
- Llamada
- Any other Falseta
- Although less common today, a silencio also serves as a nice introduction

Unlike some of the other palos, in Alegrías it is not as common to use escobilla material for your basic compás

You can use one of your less-intense llamadas to introduce a falseta. Remember, llamadas are not only used as exclamation points, but can also be great commas and periods.

The bulk of a Solo Alegrías is stringing together your falsetas in an artful way. The more varied the compás in between falsetas is the more cohesive your solo will be. You can play as many or few falsetas as you think will best engage your audience.

If you have enough material for a 12-minute Alegrías, think about doing two 6-minute ones instead.

End on 10!

It is OK to have a less intense llamada as your final closure. We don't always have to end with a bang.

Chapter 1 • Bulerias

FLAMENCO EXPLAINED

Bulerías is at once one of the lightest and most fun of the *palos,* but also one of the most difficult to master. While on paper Bulerías is nothing more than a faster version of Soleá, the groove is entirely different. It tends to incorporate more rhythmic possibilities and is often played at breakneck speeds, making it considerably more challenging.

While Bulerías is its own individual *palo*, it is also used at the end of most of the other 12-beat palos – as they build in tempo until they work their way into the tempo (and feel) of Bulerías. A typical tempo range for Bulerías is from around 160 BPM to around 275 BPM (we've all gone even faster, but no one expects you to play anything too fancy at the fastest tempos). Once a *palo* arrives at the Bulerías tempo, there is often a sense of the rhythm "flipping" – on paper nothing changes, but the groove changes and beat 12 becomes a strong downbeat, and the true beginning of the *compás*.

The Bulerías *compás* is also the most flexible of the twelve-beat *palos*. It can be felt in a variety of ways, but the two most common are given here:

Accent Pattern 1

12 1   2   **3**   4   5   **6**   7   **8**   9   **10** 11

Accent Pattern 2

12 1   2   **3**   4   5   6   **7** **8**   9   **10** 11

Beats 3 and 10 are the strongest accents in both of the above grooves, mainly because the chords change on those beats. Yet beat 12 continues to serve as the downbeat, or "start," of the *compás*. Like Soleá and Alegrías, you will learn to form complete *compases* by mixing and matching the separate halves of the *compás*.

Bulerías is one of the most difficult, but also most rewarding *palos* in flamenco. Have fun!

Basic Compás

Here are both accent patterns with some basic chords before you encounter the two separate halves of the *compás* (like you saw with Alegrías and Soleá), which you will mix and match to construct your own.

Accent Pattern I

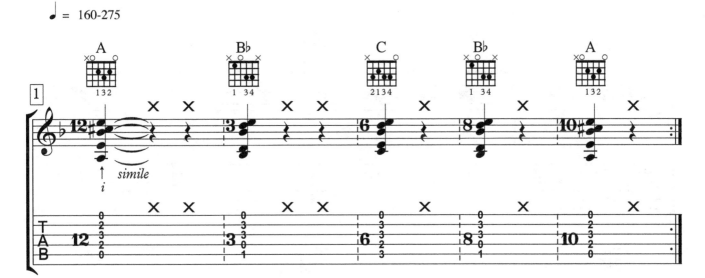

Accent Pattern 2

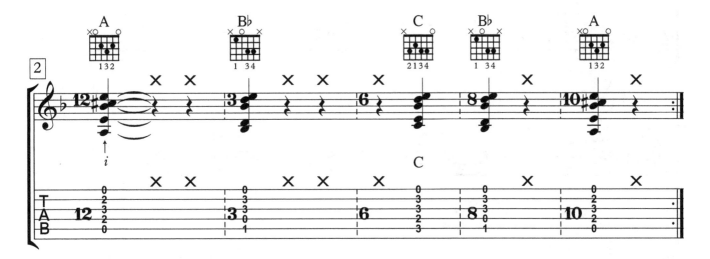

Bulerías: Beats 12-5

Bulerías: Beats 6-11

Bulerías: Complete Compases

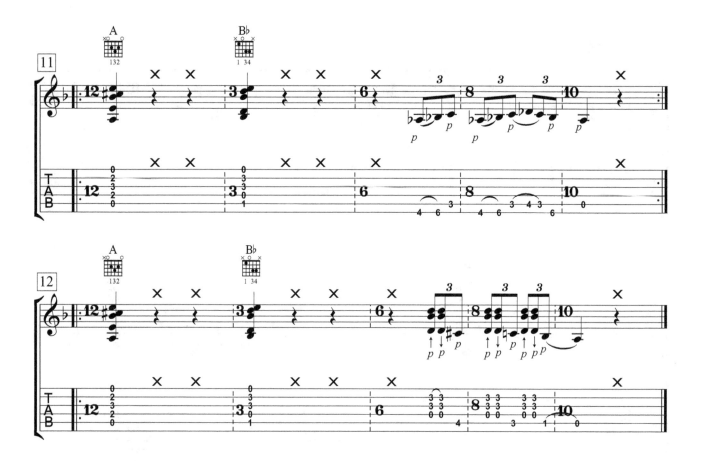

Basic Compás: More Advanced

This is correct, it is just syncopated by ending just before beat 10!

Endings in Bulerías

Bulerías closures can be many lengths and have almost limitless variations. We have provided a few single-*compás* closures here, along with two which take multiple *compases* to complete. You will notice that the longer closures begin with regular *compás,* and then begin their actual drive to closure on beat 10. You should strive to increase volume and intensity over the course of the closure for maximum effect.

Single-Compás Closures

Extended Closure 1

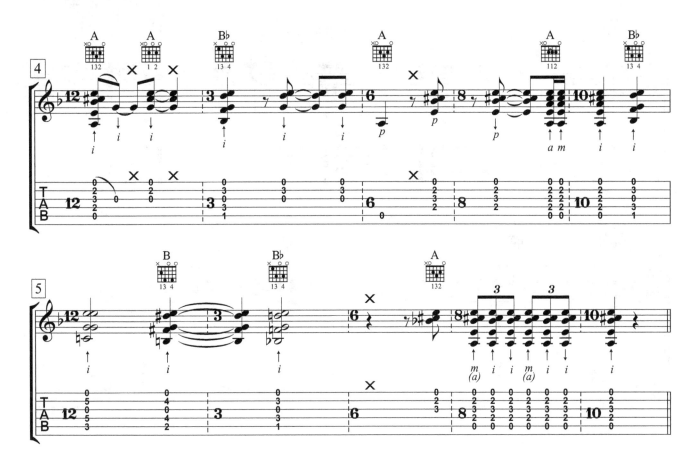

Extended Closure 2

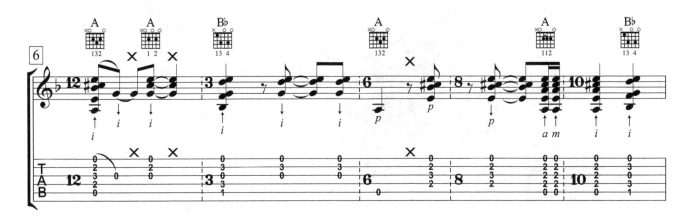

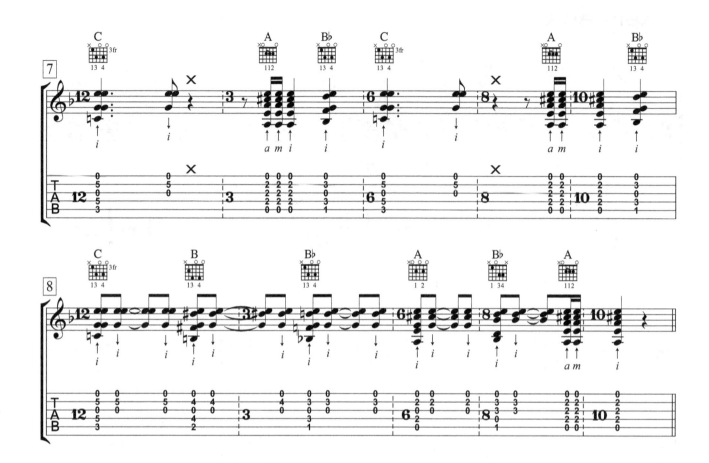

Falseta 5.4: More Thumb

Notes: This is a fairly traditional sounding *falseta* that will give you a chance to get accustomed to the feel of Bulerías. This *falseta* is also a good workout for the right-hand thumb and therefore should help to improve your *alzapua*.

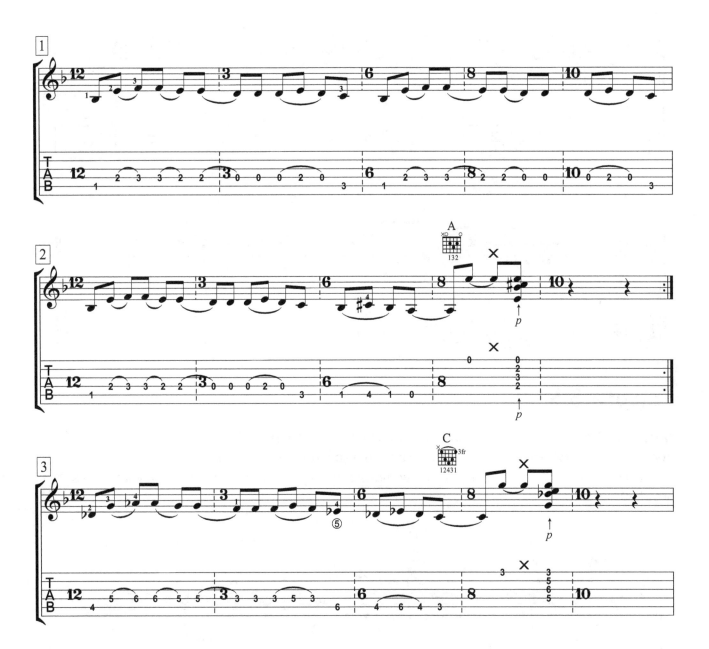

Falseta 5.5

Notes: Any basic compás phrase will work from beats 12-10 here, as long as your hands are free to begin the *falseta* just after beat 10. You can also string together *falseta* 5.4 and 5.5 by beginning 5.5 just after beat 10, in the fifth compás of 5.4 - you may have noticed the initial notes are identical.

Falseta 5.5 really begins here

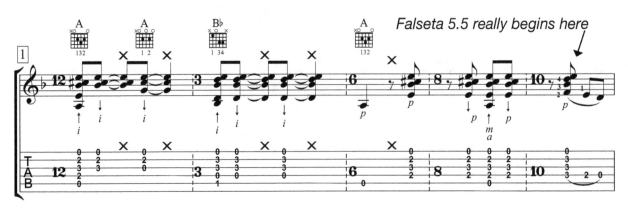

Falseta 5.6: An Important Rhythmic Device

This falseta is a great example of something that happens all the time in Bulerías - a three note arpeggio played in 8th notes. i.e., two notes to a beat but your ear will hear groupings of three. The result is that the first note of each arpeggio alternates between falling on a downbeat and falling on an upbeat. The trick is to distinguish between the downbeat (a factor of time) and the arpeggio (a factor of technique) to achieve a phrasing appropriate to Bulerías. You will be playing two three-note arpeggios for every six beats, and this is the feel we are going for.

Once you've mastered this, you'll see that you can accent either the first beat of each group of three (as in the first half of a Bulerias compás) or the first beat of each group of two (as in the second half of the Buleris compás). Either way will work, but they will groove differently, so be sure to choose your groove and not simply allow the technical aspects to dictate the rhythm you are playing.

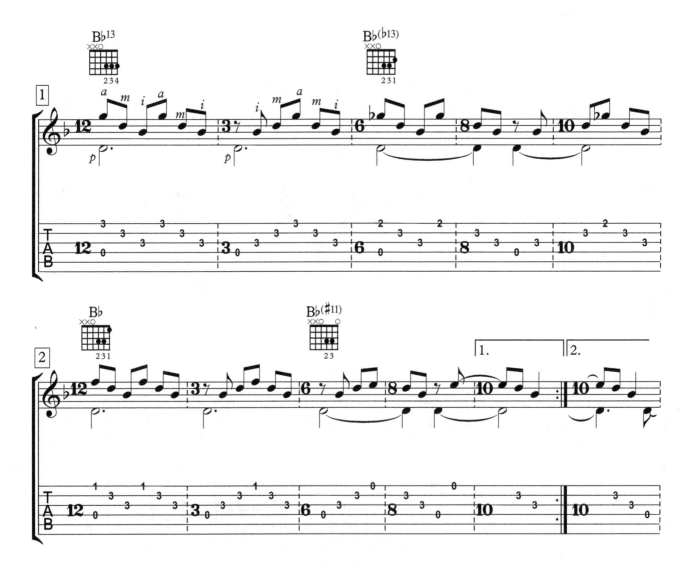

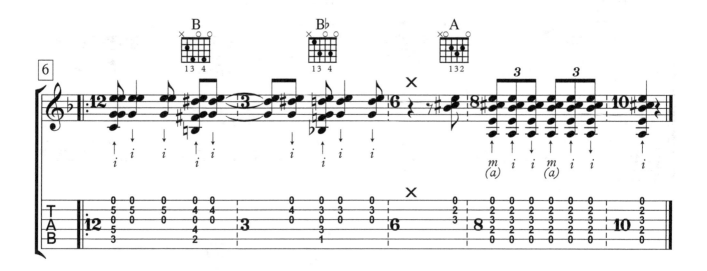

Bulerías: Constructing a Solo

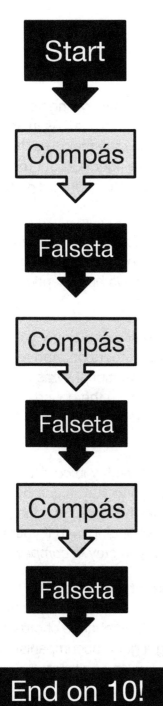

(Pick any of these)
- Intro Falseta
- Llamada
- Any other Falseta
- Tapado compás is also a nice way to set your groove

As you may have noticed, there is a pattern to most solo flamenco guitar! If we have to boil it down, it's probably this: find a nice way to string together compás and falsetas. A nice intro and ending are icing on the cake.

Chapter 6 • Accompaniment

FLAMENCO
EXPLAINED

The art of accompanying flamenco begins with the singer. Accompanying singers is not easy, but neither is it quite as mysterious as some might make it out to be. As in any other music, the goal is simply to play the appropriate chords to accompany the melodies that are being sung. The difficulty comes as a result of not knowing what the singer is about to sing, but as you listen to more *cante,* you'll begin to hear that certain melodies and chord progressions are used frequently, and soon your ears will acclimate.

Rather than trying to memorize all of the possible *letras* in a given *palo,* the trick is to familiarize yourself with the melodies and cadences. The more you listen, the more you'll realize that the majority of *letras* in a given *palo* follow certain patterns. There will always be exceptions, but with time you will train your ears to follow these too.

As in any style, there is no substitute for experience, and in the absence of a singer you may want to play along with CDs or YouTube videos to get a feel for what others do. And remember that in "real life" (i.e., at most tablao gigs) the singers will sing more traditional *letras* than what you hear from modern recordings. After all, recording artists tend to push the boundaries and even invent original *letras,* whereas most *tablao* gigs will feel more like sitting in with a band playing covers.

At first, you'll want to master a few right-hand patterns so that you can stay in *compás* while your ears follow the melodies. The more you can trust your right hand to stay in *compás,* the easier it will be for you to follow along. You'll find that the singer may need you to change chords at a point in the *compás* where you are not accustomed to changing, and if your right hand can stick to an almost automatic pattern this can greatly help you stay in *compás.*

As an accompanying guitarist you'll want to be careful not to interrupt the singer. Don't assume the singer wants you to play a *falseta* after every *letra,* and don't try to anticipate what the singer is about to sing if you're not familiar with them (it's better to be late than change chords before your singer does). A little modesty can go a long way in becoming a good accompanist and you will probably find that a good singer can be as important a teacher as any guitarist.

You're more likely to find a dance studio that will allow you to hone your accompaniment skills sitting in on dance classes than you are to find a singer who would do the same. For this reason, many of us begin with accompanying dance. When it comes to dance, the best thing you can do is stay in *compás* and learn to recognize *llamadas.*

For examples of everything in this chapter go to FlamencoExplained.com.

Accompanying 6.1: Cante in Tangos

Tangos is a nice *palo* to start with as the ⁴⁄₄ time will make life a little easier. Still, we are going to practice keeping a simple right-hand pattern going to facilitate listening for the chord changes (rather than worrying about rhythm). For now we will only vary the right hand for the *llamadas*. In time, as the various right-hand patterns become interchangeable for you, you will find you are free to choose whichever patterns seem to suit the music best in that moment.

The *letra* we are using here is often referred to as Triana (because the lyrics refer to Triana, the traditionally gypsy barrio of Sevilla), though in fact there are many *letras* that use this exact same melody. You'll encounter this melody with a variety of different lyrics, which is why we say that it is better to familiarize yourself with melodies and chord progressions than to specific lyrics/*letras*.

Listen for the relationship between the chords and the melodies, as you will hear variations of these in many Tangos *letras*. At the end of the *letra* you will see that the C7 resolves momentarily to F (which happens to be the relative Major of our key), and that this figure then repeats. This section of the letra is sometimes called the "*Cambio*" and is one of the more distinctive sounds in almost all of the Phrygian-key *palos*.

There are variations of the "Triana" *letra* – in one common variant the melody moves to a note that is accompanied by an E7 instead of a D-minor (or sometimes they first go to D-minor then to E7). We don't pretend to cover all of the possibilities here, but this variation is one to look out for.

Other common chords you will encounter in Tangos include E7, Gm7 and various secondary dominants (most commonly in the progression Dm, G7, C, F7, Bb, Gm, A). The more you listen to Tangos the less surprises you will run into when working with singers.

Our version of the melody of the *cante*, which you will find on the next page, is as simply realized as possible. A good singer will stick to this general melodic contour, but will embellish to taste.

If the singer pauses here, we traditionally play something that sounds like a llamada, as you can see in the guitar part below. The dancer will often do something rhythmic here too.

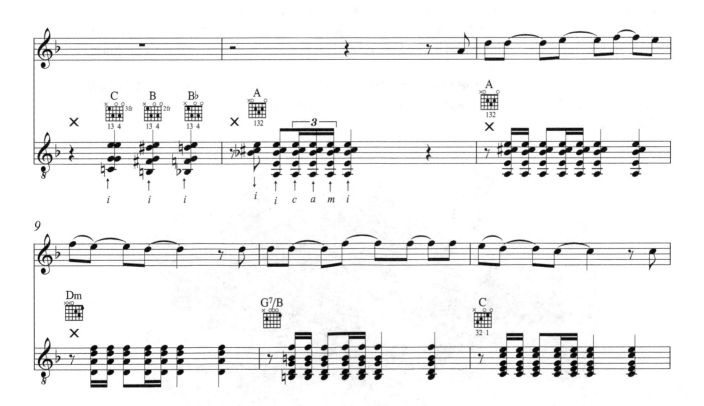

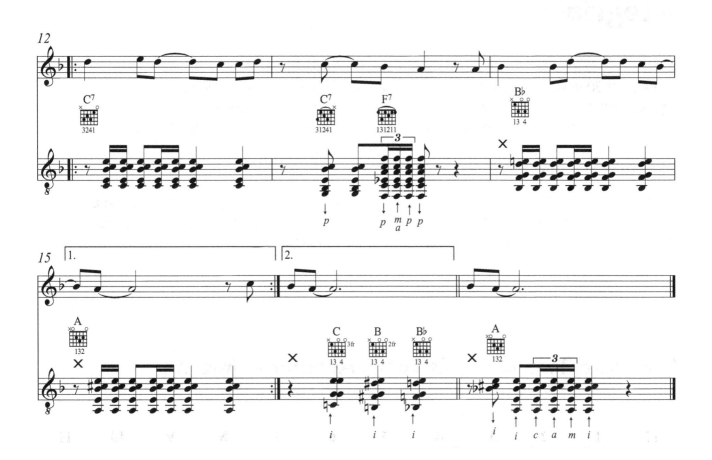

Alegrías: Accompanying Cante

In the past 30 years or so, flamenco musicians have become more exposed to other styles, such as classical music and jazz. They have discovered the many chordal variations available in tonal harmony, and so Alegrías *letras* have evolved immensely. But, at the *tablao*, the vast majority of *letras* will still follow a very predictable pattern utilizing a simple harmonic accompaniment.

Singers will most often begin their *letras* on, or around, beat 1 in Alegrías. After singing a single *compás* opening (which moves from E to B7 on beat 3, and back to E on beat 10), the singer will move into a two-*compás* pattern that works like this:

Standard Two-Compás Letra Accompaniment

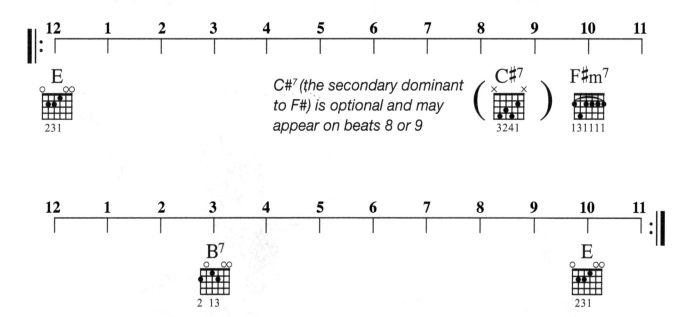

This two-compás pattern can repeat anywhere from two to ten (or more) times, depending on the length of the letra desired by either the singer or the dancer.

Here is a simple written-out accompaniment using the chord changes discussed on page 94.

Single-Compás Opening

Standard Two-Compás Accompaniment

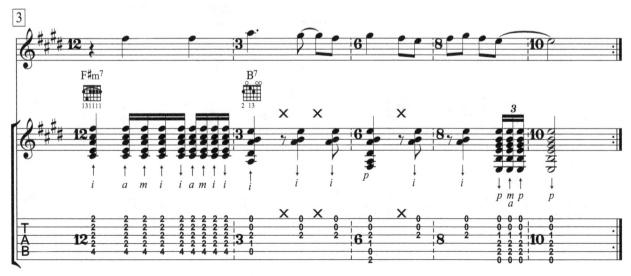

Here is a more advanced sample accompaniment, again using the chord changes discussed on page 94.

Accompanying 6.3: Additional Cante

In addition to the *letra*, we must learn the "Tiri-ti-tran" and the *coletilla*, which are not technically *letras*, but are sung sections commonly found in Alegrías. These melodies function a bit differently than the standard *letra*. The *coletilla* tends to be "tacked on" to the end of the *letra*. It typically begins on the upbeat to beat 11 in the last *compás* of the *letra*, and this upbeat helps to signal that the *coletilla* melody is about to be sung.

While the *coletilla* begins before the end of the *compás*, you can think of it as a long pickup to beat 12, which is the first strong beat of the *coletilla*. As an accompanist you will play the same two-*compás* pattern as the standard *letra*, but the feel of the *compás* is slightly different (we're definitely starting on 12 in this case), while the chords change in the same places.

The "Tiri-ti-tran" is named for the syllables the singer sings with this melody. It is identical in feel, melody, and harmony to the typical *coletilla*, and may be used in place of the *coletilla*. It is most often used as a *salida* to the *cante* for danced Alegrías, or for a *cante* solo.

The main thing to grasp here is that the two melodies and their accompaniment are essentially the same, the difference being the way the singer and guitarist enter:

- The "Tiri-ti-tran's" can begin at the end of a *letra*, after a *llamada*, or basic *compás* (as in our example on page 99).

- The *coletilla* is attached to the end of the *letra*, and so the singer sings a pickup in the last *compás* of the *letra* to signal the *coletilla's* beginning (see example below).

Pick-up notes are tacked on to signal the beginning of the coletilla here

Final Compás of the Standard Letra going to the *coletilla*

"Tiri-ti-tran" begins with basic *compás*

Both "Tiri-ti-tran" and *coletilla share this melody*

Cante and Baile: The Castellana

The Castellana is a section that typically comes after the Silencio. The dancer marks a strong 1, 2, 3, to begin a one-*compás llamada* and then the singer launches into a up-tempo *coletilla* melody. The Castellana will generally come to a complete halt (most likely with a *llamada*) at the end of the *coletilla* and the dancer will then begin the *escobilla*.

Generally we have a couple choices of how to accompany the dancer's 1-2-3 entrance into the Castellana. We want to copy the dancer's rhythm as closely as possible here. If you know your dancer well, you can come in directly with him or her. If not, we can wait for those three strong beats and enter on beat 4.

Here are two examples of a likely rhythm and accompaniment for the *llamada* beginning the Castellana:

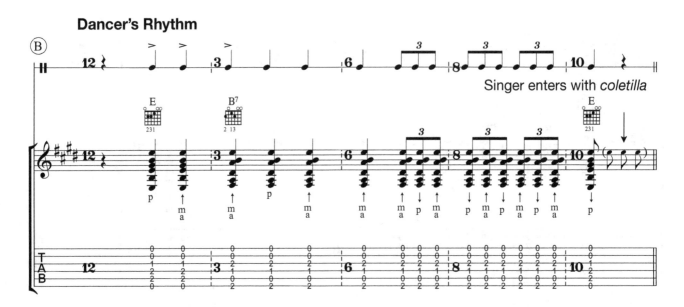

Baile in Alegrías: Escobilla

In a typical *escobilla*, phrases will be arranged in a two-*compás* pattern that, unlike usual *compás*, waits until beat 10 to move from E to B7, and then resolves back to E on beat 10 of the following *compás*. As in Soleá, the guitarist needs to provide a clear pulse for the dancer to follow, and the melodies are again divided into three-beat groups. You will notice that each *compás* begins on beat 1.

The example below is a common melody built around the above chord changes. Once you are comfortable with this low melody, you can feel free to change the arpeggio patterns as you like. *Escobilla* in Alegrías tends to speed up, so as the tempo gets more rapid you will want your arpeggios to get more and more simple and straighforward.

Other *falsetas* can also be used to accompany an *escobilla*, just remember the bottom line: give the dancer a strong and consistent pulse!

Version A

Version B

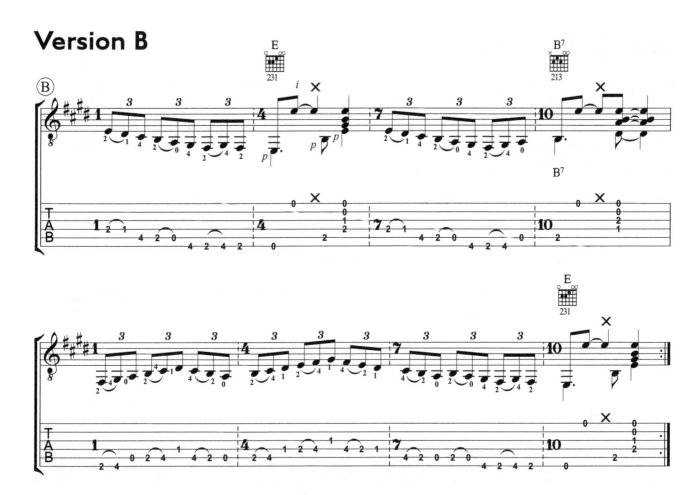

Baile in Alegrías: The Transition to Bulerías

The *escobilla* of the Alegrías will commonly build to a faster tempo before arriving at the Bulerías de Cádiz. This is one of those times when the shift between feeling groups of three (**1**-2-3, **4**-5-6, **7**-8-9, **10**-11-12) to Bulerías (**12**-1-2, **3**-4-5, **6**-7, **8**-9, **10**-11) can be confusing. We are going to call this the "flip." When *escobilla* is played very fast, with strong beats on 1, 4, 7, and 10, it can deceptively begin to feel like a Bulerías, but is still actually an *escobilla* feel – i.e., the downbeat is still 1 and not on the 12 of the Bulerías, yet.

When *escobilla* truly shifts to Bulerías it feels like changing gears. The best way to feel this is to play a strong 12 at the end of your 7, 8, 9, 10 resolution in the *escobilla*. Once you shift into Bulerías, you have two choices: you might continue to play the two-*compás* chord pattern of the escobilla as in "A" below (changing from E to B7 on beat 10, and back to E again on beat 10 of next *compás*), or you might play the single-*compás* pattern related to the Bulerías De Cádiz as in "B" on the following page (B7 on beat 3, and back to E on beat 10).

Beat 10 of the last compás of the escobilla

103

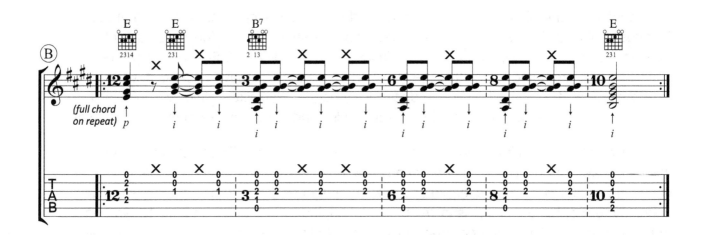

Baile in Alegrías: Bulerías de Cadiz

Because Alegrías originated in Cadiz, the Bulerías that happens at the end of the Alegrías is called the Bulerías de Cádiz. The Bulerías de Cádiz is played in the Bulerías *compás*, but played in the major key of the Alegrías, in this case E-major.

The traditional melody and basic accompaniment for the Bulerias the Cádiz is as follows:

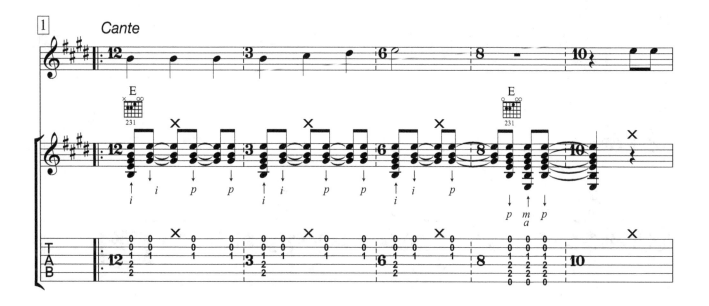

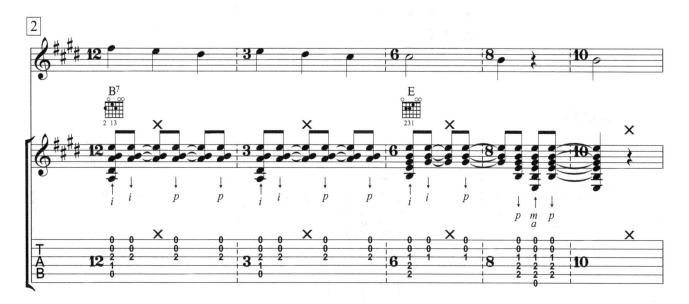

(Llamada)

Alegrías: Accompanying Baile and Cante - Structure

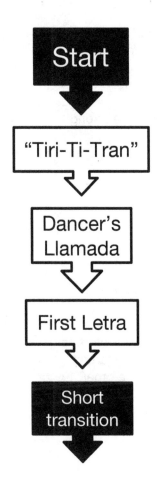

Start

(Pick any of these)
- Intro
- *Llamada*
- Intro *Falseta*
- Any other *Falseta*

"Tiri-Ti-Tran"

Could be another salida lyric, but will frequently be the same melody/chords as "Tiri-ti-tran"

Dancer's Llamada

In theory, any dance llamada will work with any guitar llamada, in practice, some work better than others, so rehearse this if possible

First Letra

This will likely fit the Alegrías standard letra

Short transition

- Often you will play a *falseta* here
- Between the *letras* you may simply return to *compás*
- You may also have a dancer's *llamada* or other footwork (*escobilla*) section
- The dancer might also proceed without this transition directly into the second *letra*

Second Letra

This will likely fit the Alegrías standard letra

Subida

*There are lots of options at this point! All these options end in a complete stop so you can begin the Silencio.

Here are some frequent ways things may proceed:

1. *Falseta* to *subida* to *llamada*
2. Subida to Closure
3. Subida to footwork (possibly *tapado*) to closure

Silencio, Then Onward!

*Some dancers will leave out the Silencio.

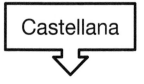

- This short *letra* seems to be falling out of fashion, so this is a great one to ask about before the show
- If your dancer chooses to skip this, simply wait until they begin the *escobilla*
- If the Castellana happens, it will end on a strong *llamada* and stop

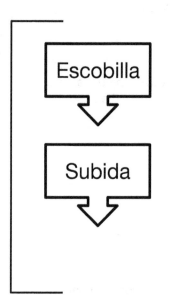

- Remember, the dancer will most likely start the *escobilla* with a very characteristic rhythmic phrase
- Parts of the *escobilla* may be *tapado*, the dancer will most likely let you know if this is the case

- The *escobilla* will gradually speed up until you reach the tempo of Bulerías
- There is always that potentially confusing moment when the feeling of the *escobilla* (starting on beat one) and the feeling of Bulerías (starting on beat twelve) will "flip" from one to the other, so watch out!
- It's not uncommon to go into a section of tapado after the 'flip'

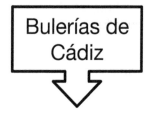

An Alegría ends one of two ways:

1. The dancer will end on stage with a strong llamada
2. The dancer will walk off the stage, or back to her seat, for which you will play a strong llamada as they exit or sit

End on 10!

By now, this probably goes without saying, but your final llamada should end on beat ten

Soleá: Accompanying Cante

First and foremost, you need to listen to as much *cante* as possible. There is simply no other way to become familiar with the music, as this is the most important element in becoming a good accompanist. As you listen, you will begin to recognize similarities among the melodies as you become more familiar with the *cante*. There is a multitude of lyrics and melodic variations in Soleá *letras*, but as an accompanist it is more important to recognize the melodies than the lyrics. Most Soleá *cante* begins with a *salida* (which can typically be accompanied by basic *compás*). There are a couple typical Soleá melodies that you should be able to recognize, and these melodies have some relatively consistent chord changes. Therefore, if you can identify which melody you are hearing, you will have greater success following the *cantaor*. We will spend quite a bit of time with Soleá *letras* because the structure, melodic shape, and chord progressions of these translate directly to Soleá por Bulerías and then to Bulerías.

Two Main Chord Progressions/Melodies

The two most common melodies (*letras*) we will encounter either begin with an ascending melody (example letra #1 ~ ascending melody) or with a repetitive note (example letra #2 ~ static melody). When the *cantaor* begins singing, we have to listen carefully in order to catch which of these two melodies he is singing. The second half of a typical letra is more predictable, as it is the same regardless of how we start the letra (ascending or repeating note). In practical terms this means that once you've identified the letra as either static or ascending, you have a pretty good sense of what you need to play.

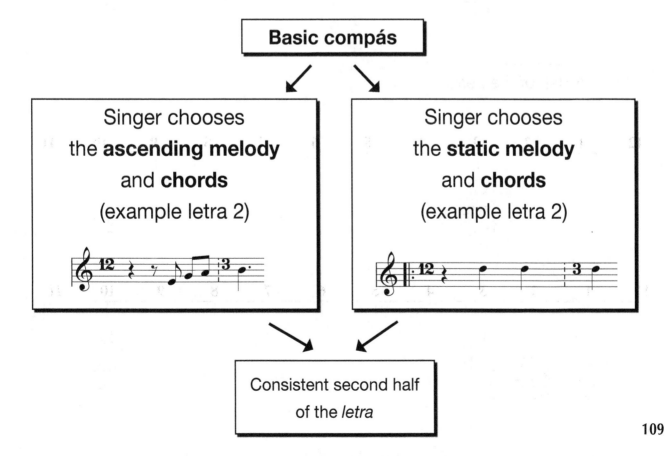

Soleá: Two Basic Melodies

Below you will find a graph of the twelve beats of the Soleá *compás* with chord charts below specific beats. When accompanying, there is a great degree of freedom for the guitarist as long as he is able to arrive on the correct chord on the right beat. Therefore we have provided this skeleton of the chord progression, with corresponding important chord arrival points, for our two common *letras*. Don't forget the second half of each melody is the same, so the chord progressions are exactly the same after you've determined if it's the ascending or static melody.

- For a possible realization of these progressions, see the example *letra* for the Ascending and Static Melodies.

- To get adjusted to the progression, you might want to simply count the *compás* and play the correct chord on the correct beat - without any added stumming or other ornamentation

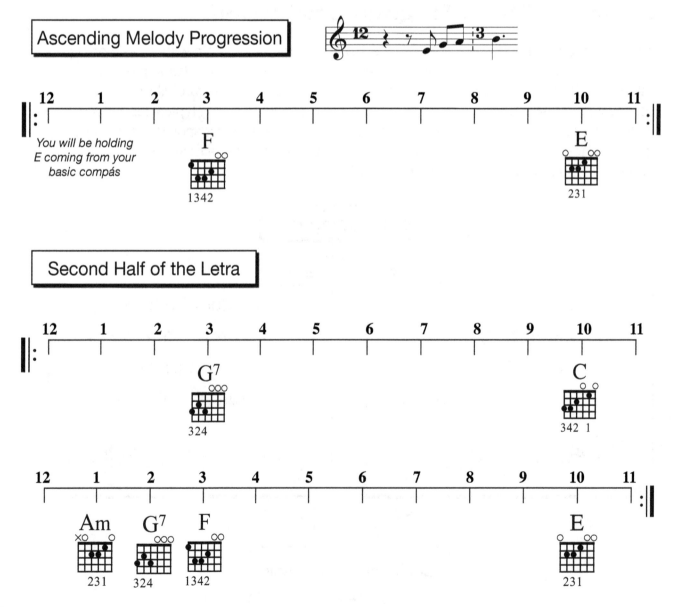

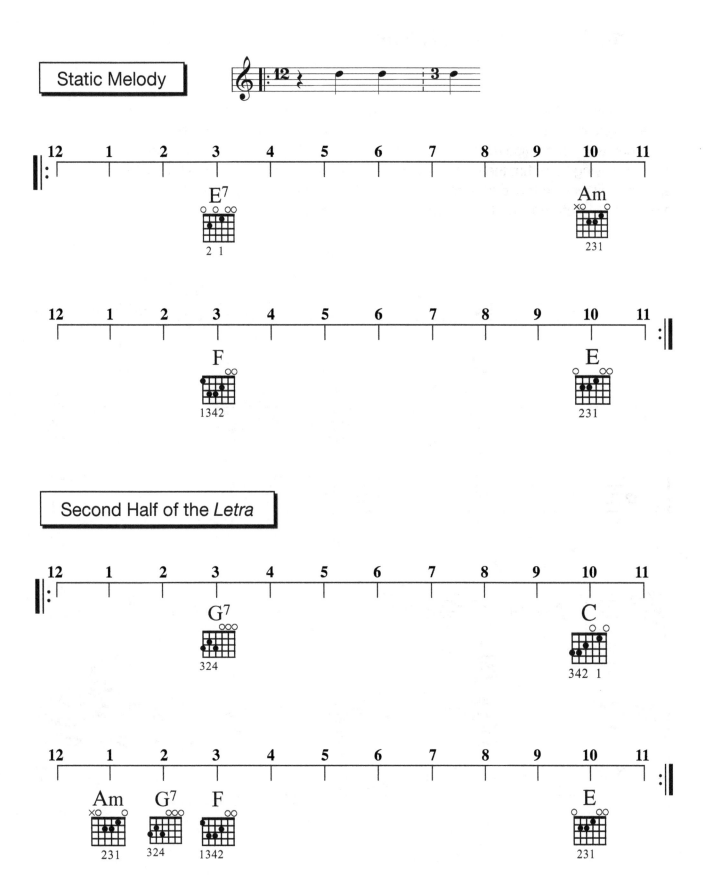

Example Letra Realization: Ascending Melody

Notes: In the first example you may notice that the first part of the *letra* is not literally repeated - this is because while the chord structure is the same, the guitarist can constantly improvise rhythms, chord voicings, etc. Don't forget that you are accompanying, and that the singer needs to be the center of focus - Don't steal the spotlight by playing too loud or too many notes! And lastly, during the cante, Soleá is not meant to be metronomic - try to let the singer guide the rhythm.

Cante/Voice

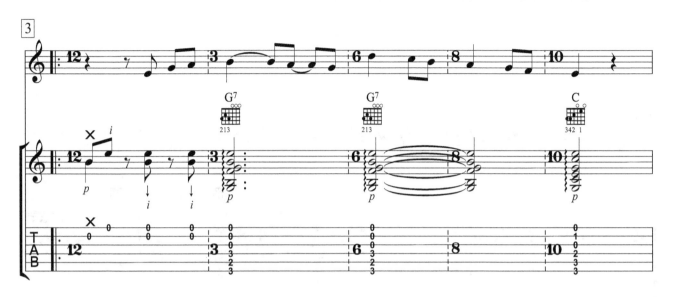

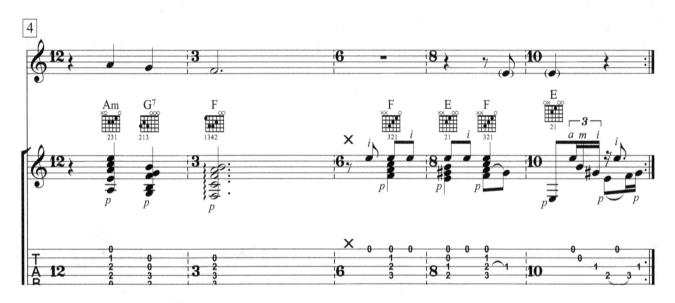

Example Letra Realization: Static Melody

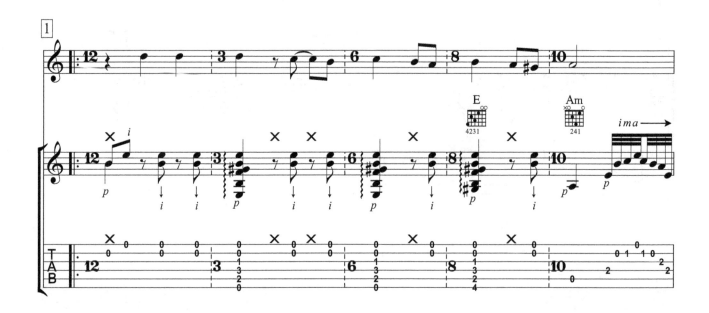

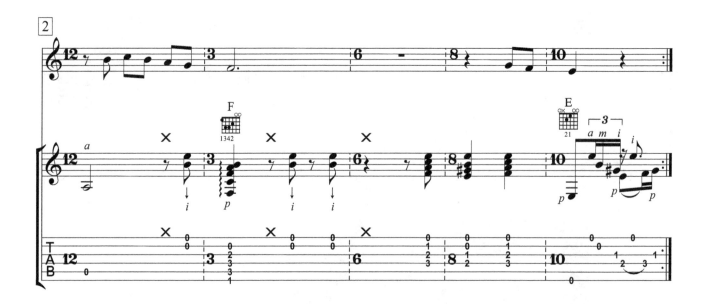

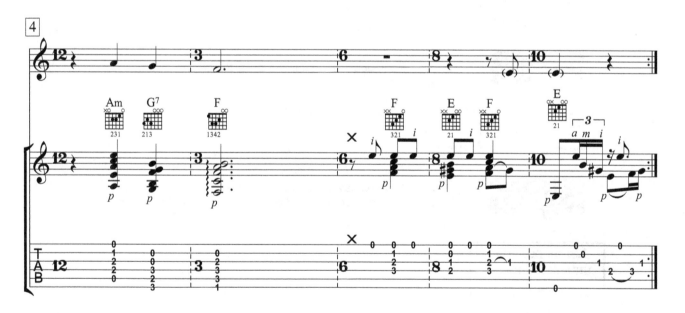

Soleá: Accompanying Cante - Structure

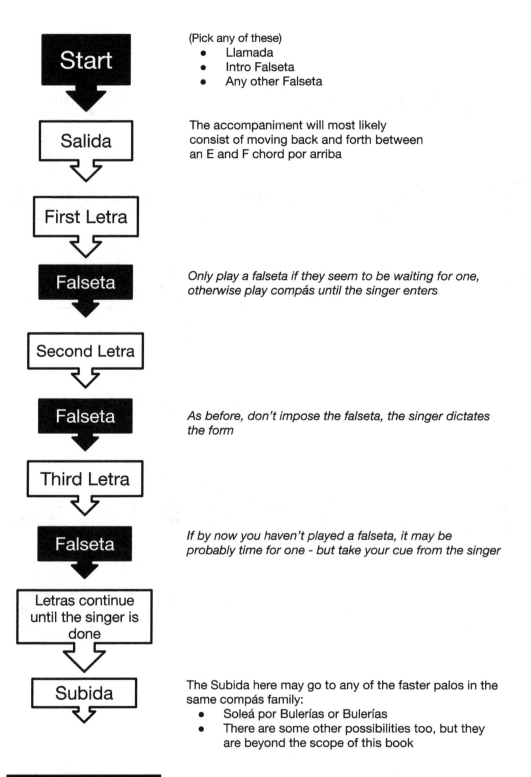

Start — (Pick any of these)
- Llamada
- Intro Falseta
- Any other Falseta

Salida — The accompaniment will most likely consist of moving back and forth between an E and F chord por arriba

First Letra

Falseta — *Only play a falseta if they seem to be waiting for one, otherwise play compás until the singer enters*

Second Letra

Falseta — *As before, don't impose the falseta, the singer dictates the form*

Third Letra

Falseta — *If by now you haven't played a falseta, it may be probably time for one - but take your cue from the singer*

Letras continue until the singer is done

Subida — The Subida here may go to any of the faster palos in the same compás family:
- Soleá por Bulerías or Bulerías
- There are some other possibilities too, but they are beyond the scope of this book

End on 10! — *Always end with your strongest llamada*

Soleá: Accompanying both Cante and Baile

Playing with Dance

Generally when Soleá is danced, we can expect to incorporate many of the sections we have already learned for solo playing as well as those we have learned for accompying *cante*. The interaction of the *baile* and *cante* is of great importance in all danced *palos*, and so it is virtually unheard of to dance a Soleá without a singer. The emotional heart of the dance is essentially a response to what is being sung. The only time the *cante* is not the center of focus in a Soleá is during the footwork sections like the *escobilla*, which highlight the dancer's technical prowess.

In addition to our basic *compás*, *letras*, and *falsetas*, the sections that are particular to the dance will probably begin with an *escobilla*, then go into a faster form called Soleá Por Bulería. The Soleá Por Bulería section is essentially a faster-tempo version of the normal Soleá, with a slightly different feel (the groove is in fact identical to what we learned for Alegrías, though the tonality is that of Soleá). For our purposes, you can use Soleá for this section and you can expect to hear a different tempo and feel. After the *letra*, the dancer can choose to do more footwork with *escobilla* accompaniment, or to speed up using the *subida* step.

Over the course of the Soleá, the dancer will probably speed things up gradually until reaching the tempo and feel of Bulerías. 12-beat *compás* dances tend to end up at Bulería tempo, and at some point during the acceleration you will feel the shift from the three-beat groups of *escobilla* to the 12-beat-oriented feel. The Bulería section can vary substantially, as you may find additional *letras*, footwork, *falsetas*, etc. Here we give several *compases* in order for you to get a feel for how the music changes at a faster tempo and a closure to end the piece.

117

Soleá: Escobilla for Baile

Notes: *Compases* one and two are individual units and can each be repeated, or played back to back, as many times as you would like. The third and fourth *compases* should be played as a single, two-*compás* unit (phrase).

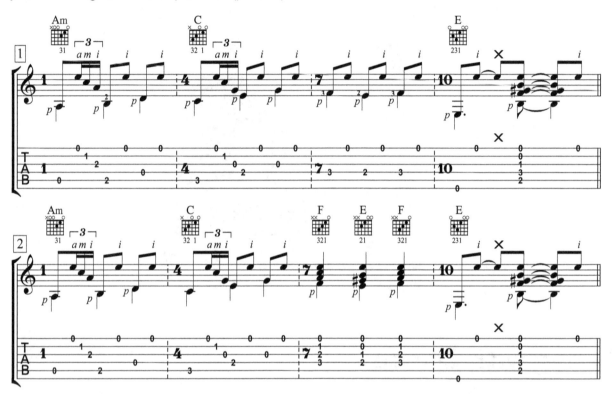

Two-Compás Phrase

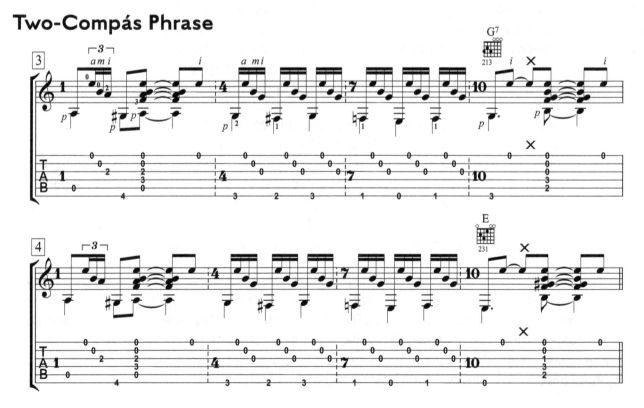

Soleá: The Subida to Bulerías

The Subida - Speeding Up

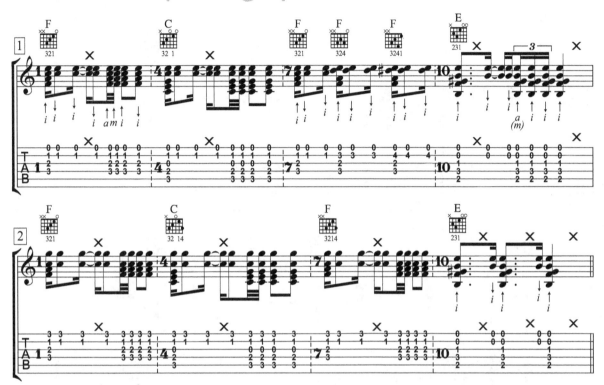

The "Flip" - Switching to the 12-Beat Feel of Bulerías

This can be a tricky moment! At some point during the *subida*, the dancer will begin accenting the 12-beat cycle (beats 12-3-6-8-10) with her heelwork. While it is best if you can change immediately when she does, you do not have to. But once you realize the dancer has made this shift, you should make the transition within the next *compás* or two. You can do this by playing a simple few chords beginning on beat 7, as you can see in the example below. Beat 12 of the *subida* will then become the beginning of the Bulerías phrase on page 120.

This is now the beginning of your Bulerías phrase

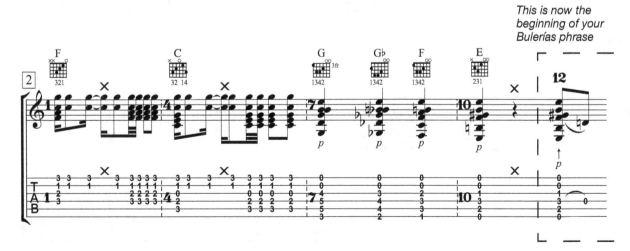

Soleá: Bulerías Tempo

*Begins with beat 12 from the
the subida on page 119.*

(Closure)

Soleá: Accompanying Cante and Baile - Structure

While this structure might seem straightforward on paper, in practice each individual section has its own challenges, and the transitions from one section to another can be unpredictable. The best way to become familiar with these transitions, and the overall structure of this dance, is to experience and study as much flamenco as possible. Seeing flamenco live is the best option but YouTube can be a good substitute!

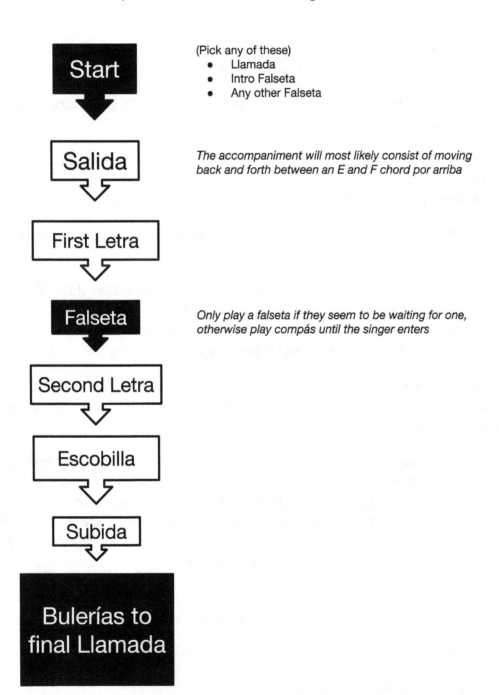

Start — (Pick any of these)
- Llamada
- Intro Falseta
- Any other Falseta

Salida — *The accompaniment will most likely consist of moving back and forth between an E and F chord por arriba*

First Letra

Falseta — *Only play a falseta if they seem to be waiting for one, otherwise play compás until the singer enters*

Second Letra

Escobilla

Subida

Bulerías to final Llamada

* The danced Soleá usually includes a section called Soleá por Bulería which we have omitted here. This is a topic that goes beyond the scope of this text. Go to FlamencoExplained.com to learn more.

Parting Words: At the Tablao Gig

Let's imagine a hypothetical situation (which is actually a very real one for most working guitarists) – you arrive at your gig and find that there is a new dancer with whom you've never worked, and you have to perform in 15 minutes. How do you find out what you need to know to accompany that dancer well? The most important thing for a well-prepared guitarist is to understand the structure of the dancer's solo. Asking the following questions will give you a quick understanding of the overall structure of most dances:

How do we start? – Often a dance solo will begin with a guitar intro (falseta), but it can also begin with a Salida de cante, or the dancer could even begin the dance without music

How many letras? – Since a dance will often change after the last letra, it's very important to know how many letras the dancer wants to dance.

What happens between letras? – The dancer may want a falseta between the letras, or after the last letra, so it's good to ask. If you don't have a falseta you can just play compás, but make sure to tell the dancer so that they don't wait for you to start a falseta you're not going to play.

Then what? – Generally after the last letra you can expect an escobilla, a subida, or possibly a footwork section in which the guitar plays tapado.

The danced Alegria has a few specific sections that are unique – **Is there a Silencio? A Castellana? Does the escobilla start in simple or double time?** I generally ask to see the first three beats of the escobilla just to be sure, and remember that dancers don't always share a vocabulary with musicians, so to be extra sure I may ask them to sing the escobilla melody while dancing the first compás.

Anything else I need to know? A dancer may be used to working with musicians who know the dancer's choreography very well, so it's always good to ask if there's anything in particular that the dancer wants you to know about.

Breaks, or kicks, or hits - dancers will often incorporate dramatic rhythmic breaks on normally un-accented beats, which can be particulary effective when synchronized with the musicians. For a well-rehearsed show, you should learn them all. At a tablao gig, they may ask you to learn twenty of these five minutes before the show, but you can't be expected to learn every break. However, if you have a few minutes before the show begins and you are already comfortable with the structure of all the dances you are playing that night, you may want to learn one or two.

In time, you probably won't need to ask as many questions - you'll find you develop an intuition for the structure, and don't be surprised if the dancer whispers, or even shouts instructions on stage.

Don't forget, you can also check FlamencoExplained.com for additional resources!

Mucha mierda! (Good luck! And don't break a nail!)

Glossary

We have gone out of our way in this book to use as few "technical," or simply untranslatable, terms as possible. There is a very specific reason for this: flamenco guitarists, singers, and dancers too often use different words to mean the same thing. Since a large part of this book is about successfully communicating in the flamenco environment, we encourage you not to get hung up on terms. The most important thing is to understand, and to be understood, in the most efficient way we can. As soon as you are on the same page with the rest of the group (singers, dancers, percussionists, other guitarists, bass players, keyboard players, flautists, we could go on...), you've won! Here is a list of generally agreed upon terms that will appear frequently in this book. You can find additional detail and demonstrations of these concepts, and more, at *FlamencoExplained. com*.

Alzapúa – A technique unique to flamenco in which the thumb is used like a guitar pick to alternately strum and play single notes, usually with melodies in the bass.

Arpeggio - A guitar technique using the fingers of the right hand to play the notes of a chord in sequence rather than simultaneously.

Baile - Dance.

Cante - Cante means song or singing. A *Cantaor/a* is a flamenco singer.

Compás – This word has many meanings: See our section on *compás*.

Estribillo – A chorus as sung by the cantaor or played by musicians.

Falseta – A self-contained melodic idea, usually written by the guitarist, that can be as many *compáses* long as the player desires.

Golpe – A percussive strike on the body of the guitar.

Letra – A verse of flamenco *cante*, often self-contained and not necessarily related to the other *letras* in a song.

Llamada – Literally, the word "llamada" means call in Spanish. *Llamadas* are a little tricky to define, as they fall under the old adage "I know them when I hear/see them." They are a short (one or two compás) declaration of the essense of the *compás* (of whichever *palo* -see below- is being played). Dancers and musicians use them to open and close sections, to call the attention of the other artists on stage, or to otherwise punctuate musical ideas. Each *palo* has its traditional *llamadas*, and artists will often create their own variations of these. You will find various examples of *llamadas* for each of the palos explored in this book.

> You are also going to need to learn to recognize dancers' *llamadas* which are used to call your attention, and honestly the best way to learn to recognize them is by playing for dance class and accompanying as much as possible. It's interesting to note that singers do not sing *llamadas*, instead they respond to them.

Macho – Occassionally at the end of a piece (solo guitar, *cante*, or dance), the artist will transition to a faster version of the current *palo* (see below). Sometimes this means a change in the groove, or even a change to the parallel major key. For example, tientos will have tangos as its *macho*, tangos will have rumba as its *macho*. Similarly, twelve-beat *palos* will have bulerías as their *macho*.

Palmas – The rhythmic handclaps that accompany flamenco, and the earliest form of flamenco percussion. Don't underestimate the importance of *palmas* (and don't assume you can do them without practice!). See

Glossary (cont.)

FlamencoExplained.com for lots more information about *palmas*.

Palo – Literally meaning 'branch', the *palos* are the forms in flamenco, like Soleá, Buleria, etc… and are seen as the branches of the tree of flamenco.

A palo seco – Synonym for "tapado."

Patada – a short little flourish of footwork. *Patadas* are often valued for their creativity as much as, or more, than for their technical prowess.

Picado – Rest-stroke scales in flamenco.

Por fiesta – This is loosely translated "as at a party," and is a looser, less structured way of dancing and playing. Bulerías, Tangos, and Rumbas are the *palos* most often danced *por fiesta*, and dancers take turns dancing to one *letra* of *cante* often followed by a *patada*. You'll often see non-dancers (i.e. musicians and non-professionals) dance *por fiesta*.

Rasgueado – Flamenco strumming – any time you use the back of the nails of your fingers (not your thumb) to play a note. It's easiest to grasp through a video, so you might just go visit FlamencoExplained.com and watch Kai's "Introduction to Rasgueado" video. In the meantime, and if you are new to rasgueado technique, there are a couple quick suggestions we can make here to get you started.

> Flick out each finger as if you are flicking a bug off your knee. We are trying for individual, percussive, and rhythmic strokes with each finger, rather than just unfurling your fingers in a blur of sound.

> We prepare our rasgueados by making a loose fist. The fist allows us to "cock" (prepare) each finger to fire. The idea being that your finger is being shot out of the fist, rather than pushing through the strings.

> The hand is supported by the thumb which rests on the sixth string. You will find that a bent first thumb-joint will allow for a better angle to attack the strings (especially the 5th string, which is so important to so many chord voicings in flamenco).

Salida – Generally the first part of the *Cante* that is sung to call out the dancer or introduce the dance or the *cante*. The salida will generally be a loose melody on syllables such as "ay" and can often be accompanied by basic compás.

Solo de pie – Literally 'foot solo', this is a section where the dancer shows off their footwork, sometimes performed without accompaniment from the guitarist.

Subida – Literally a 'lift', a *subida* is a quickening of tempo, which can be gradual or sudden.

Tablao – Used as a noun, a *tablao* is a club where you might see flamenco performed. As an adjective, *tablao* is used to denote informality and a more improvised style of performance.

Tapado – Playing the guitar as a percussion instrument by muting the strings with the left hand.

Tonic – The tonic is the first note of the scale used to build a piece of music. This note, and corresponding chord, gives us a sense of resolution in music. We often refer to this as "home base." For example, in the key of A, the root of the main chord is A, therefore tonic is A.

Flamenco Chord Voicings

One of the most distinctive things about flamenco is the particular sound of the voicings used on the guitar. Many of the voicings used don't analyze very easily, yet are very comfortable to play and sound great! The guitar being the first harmonic accompaniment to flamenco, the instrument itself is partly responsible for these characteristic sonorities, as many of the harmonies simply incorporate the open strings into the chord voicing. This often adds notes that are not necessarily found in other musical styles.

For this reason, Western analysis of these voicings can lead to overly complicated names. To simplify we have grouped them by function. In practical terms, this means that when you encounter the chord A, you are free to use virtually any of the versions we have provided here, or that you have learned along the way.

If you recognize a voicing as something you are already familiar with, but you know it with a different name or function, you are probably right. Don't let this confuse you. In flamenco, it just makes more sense to think in terms of chord function, in other words an A is an A no matter which voicing or added notes you may encounter, add, or even invent. Therefore, we name chords according to their function rather than their voicing, so F9(#11) is just F, because the function of F is the same regardless of any extra "color" notes.

It's difficult to think about key in flamenco because we use the capo so often - as in much folk music, these guitar voicings are part of the essential sound of flamenco, and therefore the capo is used to change keys to accommodate the singer's range, while preserving these harmonic colors. This is probably the reason you don't hear flamenco players say things like, "I want my tangos played in G#," instead, even singers will tell you where they want the capo, and which set of voicings to use. For example, "I am going to sing at the 4th fret, *por arriba*."

This brings up the two most common sets of voicings used in flamenco: *por medio* and por arriba. *Por medio* means using the voicings that correspond to the key of A-phrygian. Even if the capo is at the third fret, the voicings and left-hand shapes will be the same even though technically you are playing in C-phrygian. *Por arriba* means using the voicings that correspond to E-phrygian. The word *medio* literally means "middle" and the word *arriba* means "up," so presumably this relates to the position of the left-hand while holding an A chord (*medio*) and an E chord (*arriba*).

Common Chord Voicings Por Medio

Chords we call "A"

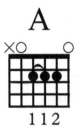
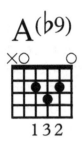
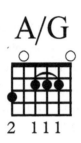
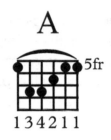
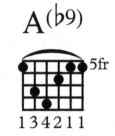

Chords we call "Bb"

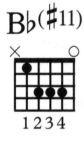
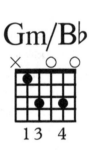
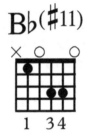

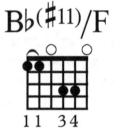

Chords we call "C"

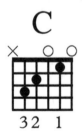
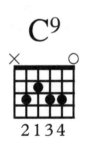
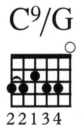
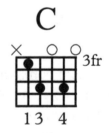
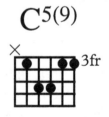

Chords we call "Dm"

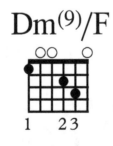
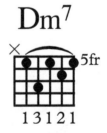
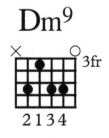

Common Chord Progressions Por Medio

1.

B♭/D   C⁹   B♭(♯11)   A(♭9)

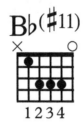

2.

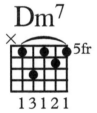

Dm⁷   C⁷   B♭⁷   A

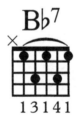

3.

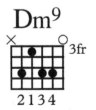

Dm⁹   C⁹   B♭(♯11)   A(♭9)

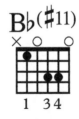

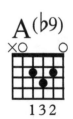

Common Chord Voicings Por Arriba

Chords we call "E"

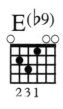

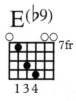

Chords we call "F"

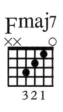
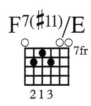

Chords we call "G"

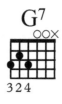

Chords we call "Am"

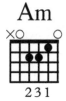
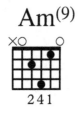
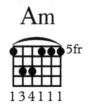
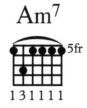
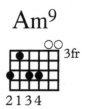

Common Chord Progressions Por Arriba

1.

 Am

 G

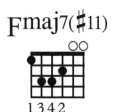 Fmaj7(♯11)

 E(♭9)

2.

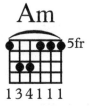 Am   G

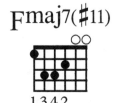 Fmaj7(♯11) E(sus4♭9)

3.

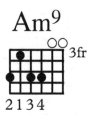 Am⁹

 G⁷

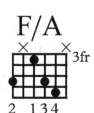 F/A

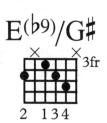 E(♭9)/G♯

A Few Warm-ups: Arpeggios for the Right Hand

These are arpeggio patterns utilizing only the open strings of the guitar. It's best to play rest-stroke (pushing through the string to land on the next) with the thumb, while the fingers play free-stroke (playing through the string into the air). Do at least four repetitions of each pattern. You can vary this warm-up in many ways, here are a few variations:

1. **Try incorporating a speed burst:** Alternate playing the patterns in quarters, as written below, then in eighths, then in sixteenths. You might want to set a metronome to your quarter note speed, then do each different duration at that tempo, in succession.

2. **Walk the thumb** across the three bass strings as you do your repetitions. For example, having the thumb play the sixth, then the fifth, then the fourth, then the fifth string is a logical pattern that ascendes up through the bass strings, and then changes direction to descend back towards the sixth string. This allows you to repeat or transition to the next pattern, without too much hopping around with the thumb.

3. Try doing the same patterns but with the fingers set on **new groups of strings**. For instance, instead of strings one, two, and three, try switching *i*, *m*, and *a* fingers to strings two, three, and four.

A Few Warm-ups: Slurs for the Left Hand

These numbers refer to pairs of left-hand fingers. These six pairs allow for all the possible left-hand finger combinations for a two-note slur.

Ascending Slurs (Hammer-ons):

1-2   2-3   3-4   2-4   1-4   1-3

Descending Slurs (Pull-offs):

2-1   3-2   4-3   4-2   4-1   3-1

This simple idea can also be expanded to a myriad of exercises, but here are two versions:

Version 1: The following slur pattern should be practiced as ascending slurs (as written), reversed for descending slurs, as well as on different strings, and in different positions on the neck.

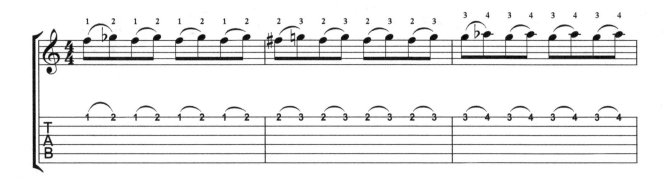

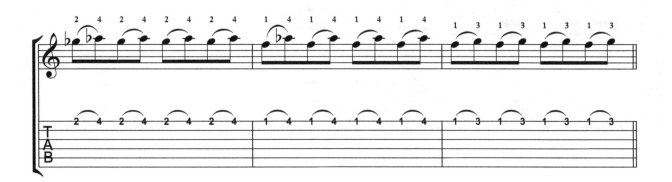

A Few Warm-ups: Slurs for the Left Hand (cont.)

Version 2: This variation is played across the strings, and combining ascending and descending slurs into a single motion. The fifth position is a nice middle ground on the neck for these, but like Version 1, they should also be practiced in various positions.

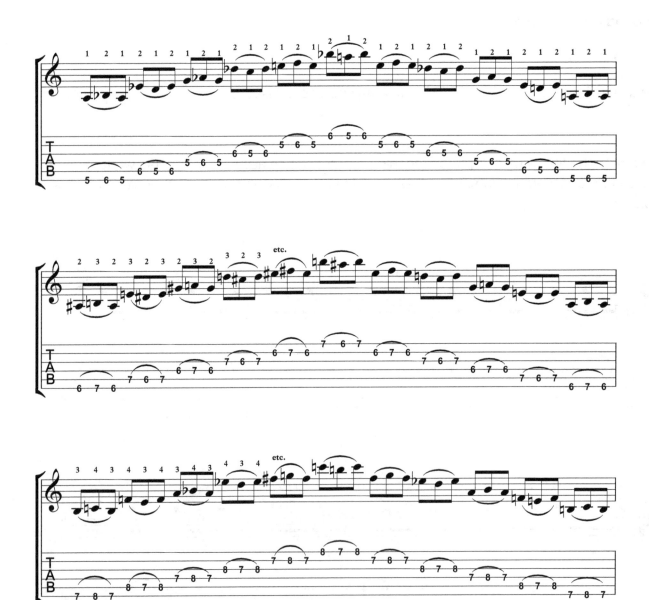

A Few Warm-ups: Slurs for the Left Hand (cont.)

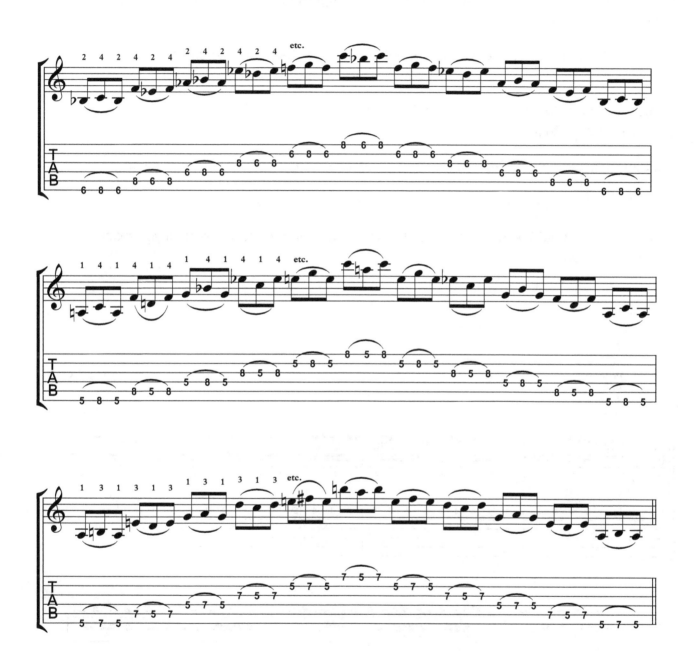

A Few Warm-ups: Left and Right Hand Coordination

This coordination exercise is nice to do both free- and rest-stroke, alternating *i-m*, *m-i*, *a-m*, *m-a*, etc. Try to focus on having both left- and right-hand fingers play at exactly the same moment.

This exercise is shown on the first string, but should, like the other exercises, be played on all strings.

A nice variation is to incorporate speed bursts into all, or parts, of the pattern once you feel familiar enough with it.

The pattern is best memorized as four groups of left-hand fingerings in one position:

1-2-3-4   4-3-2-1   1-4-3-4   2-4-3-4

Each time you repeat the left-hand pattern, move your hand a fret higher until you reach the ninth position.

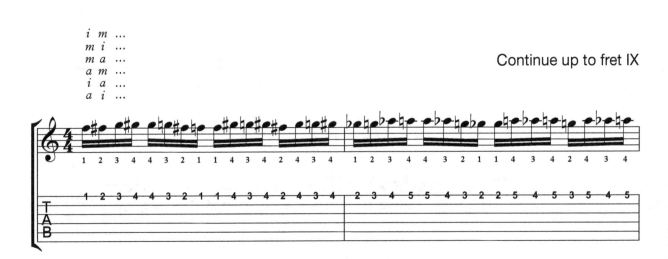

Continue up to fret IX

A Few Warm-ups: The Right-hand Thumb

Perhaps the most important difference between flamenco and classical technique is the use of the thumb. We want a much more percussive attack and sound from the thumb in flamenco. At times our thumb's movement will resemble slap technique on the bass. The power, and most of the movement, comes from rotating the forearm. Think of the motion of turning a doorknob and you'll get a good idea of how the thumb needs to move. For demonstration videos of this go to *FlamencoExplained.com*.

Rest-stroke is the default stroke for the thumb in flamenco, so do this exercise using only rest-strokes.

Do not prepare the thumb on the string you are about to play. This is a key difference between classical and flamenco. The thumb will attack from the air above the string and play all the way through it, landing on the adjacent string.

The most important thing to focus on in this repeated-note exercise is a light bounce to return the thumb to its position above the string you are about to play. Mastering this technique will help you greatly when it comes to learn *alzapúa*.

The fastest way to learn this is to see it done properly. Search for Kai's instructional video on thumb technique at *FlamencoExplained.com*.

A Few Warm-ups: The Right-hand Thumb (cont.)

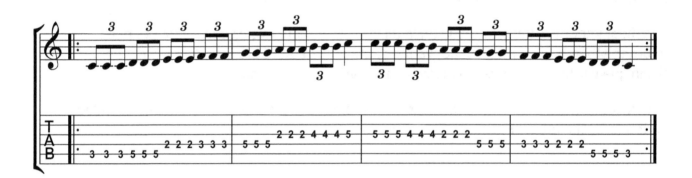

CPSIA information can be obtained
at www.ICGtesting.com
Printed in the USA
BVHW090331160122
626155BV00005B/296